The Legacy of a King

The Fourth Druk Gyalpo Jigme Singye Wangchuck

The Legacy of a King

Executive Producer	Lhatu Wangchuk
Editor/writer	Siok Sian Pek-Dorji
Editorial team	Thuji D. Nadik • Chhimmy Pem • Wangchuk • Damcho Rinzin
Design and Production	Keen Media (Thailand) Co., Ltd.

With special thanks to   Her Majesty the Queen Mother • ABTO (Association of Bhutanese Travel Operators) • Druk Air

A publication of the Department of Tourism, Royal Government of Bhutan

© Department of Tourism, Bhutan, 2007
PO Box 126, Thimphu, Bhutan
dot@tourism.gov.bt
www.tourism.gov.bt

ISBN 99936-624-6-1
Photo: cover and page 6 © Chencho Norbu • previous page Josef Polleross

𝒞ontents

A Tribute to an Enlightened Monarch

In December 2006, the fourth Druk Gyalpo, His Majesty Jigme Singye Wangchuck, handed over his responsibilities as King and Head of State to his son, Jigme Khesar Namgyel Wangchuck. The world was stunned. The Bhutanese people were overwhelmed.

Then it dawned on the people of Bhutan that the Druk Gyalpo had unravelled an enlightened vision. In this lesson of impermanence, symbolised by his final act of trust in his people, he was preparing his kingdom to withstand the challenges of the future.

Today, Bhutan and the Bhutanese people are grappling with the exhilaration and pains of forging a path to a democratic society. We understand that a new political system is as important as the need to preserve a pristine natural environment, strengthen our social, cultural and spiritual legacy, and develop a vibrant economy. We believe that the path may be difficult, but there is no other option in the search for Gross National Happiness.

The people of Bhutan, friends of Bhutan and the world media come together in this publication to acknowledge a vision that goes beyond time and to express their appreciation for the wisdom and compassion of an enlightened monarch.

This is a tribute to a king who, by placing his people and his country before himself, changed the course of history.

Chapter One

The Legacy of a King

The Legacy of a King

His Majesty King Jigme Singye Wangchuck walked away into a quiet retirement, leaving behind a story of extraordinary achievement.

Above: The young prince with his father, His Majesty Jigme Dorji Wangchuck. Opposite page: In the footsteps of his father. His Royal Highness the Crown Prince Jigme Singye Wangchuck installed as the Trongsa Penlop on March 15, 1972 in the presence of his father, the third Druk Gyalpo and His Holiness the Je Khenpo.

It was a moment in history that was as simple as it was profound. On the morning of December 14, 2006, His Majesty Jigme Singye Wangchuck issued a royal decree that declared his Crown Prince, Jigme Khesar Namgyel Wangchuck, the new King of Bhutan.

"As I hand over my responsibilities to my son, I repose my full faith and belief in the people of Bhutan, who are the true custodians of our tradition and culture, and the ultimate guardians of the security, sovereignty and continued well-being of our country," stated the decree.

Later that morning, His Majesty the fourth Druk Gyalpo, at 51 years old, left the Throne Room of Tashichhodzong from where he had conducted the affairs of state for 34 years. His Majesty walked away into a quiet retirement, leaving behind a story of extraordinary achievement that is already a legend.

Auspicious Birth

His Majesty King Jigme Singye Wangchuck was born in Dechenchholing Palace on November 11, 1955. The royal birth was a prophesy of 17th Century saint Terton Drukga Dorji, who predicted that the birth of a male heir to the throne in the Male Wood Sheep Year would bring unprecedented joy and prosperity to the Bhutanese people.

As a young prince, the heir was brought up according to the traditions of Bhutan's royal lineage, serving as an attendant in his father's court. He received his early education from private tutors, schools in India and the U.K., and the Ugyen Wangchuck Academy in Paro. He learned about the affairs of the nation by attending cabinet sessions and official meetings, and came to know the people of Bhutan through going on long

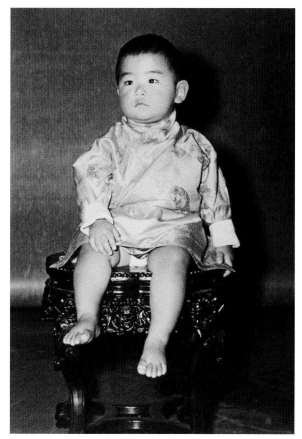

Above: The infant Crown Prince.
Opposite page: His Royal Highness the Crown Prince (front row middle) with his parents and sisters.

journeys around the country with his father, the third Druk Gyalpo.

The World's Youngest King

His Majesty Jigme Singye Wangchuck was 16 years old when he became King and the youngest monarch in the world. "It now falls upon me to join the line of dynastic succession to the throne. Since all of you have strong loyalty to me and have placed great hopes in me, for my part, I hope to serve my kingdom and its people to the best of my ability and with all my heart and soul..."

Over the next three decades, the fourth monarch of the Wangchuck dynasty took the reins of governance and steered the kingdom away from a medieval era and into a new millennium.

Bhutan cautiously opened its doors and entered the world. His Majesty had accompanied his father to India on numerous state visits and developed extremely close relationships with India's leaders over the decades. He built a strong network of friends among statesmen, politicians, diplomats, bureaucrats and journalists of diverse backgrounds and political leanings. Prime Minister Indira Gandhi said that she saw the "wisdom of centuries" in the young prince.

The Indo-Bhutan friendship matured through the decades of His Majesty's reign and came to be described as a "shining testimony of bilateral relations". India remained the largest donor to Bhutan's development efforts, and by the end of 2006, Bhutan had achieved the highest per capita income in the region. In February 2007, this friendship was symbolically consolidated in the revision of the 1949 treaty of friendship between the two countries.

From barely known, Bhutan's sovereign status grew in prominence during His Majesty's reign. While continuing to offer a hand of friendship to the world, the kingdom became a part of the global community. His Majesty led Bhutanese delegations to SAARC (South Asian Association for Regional Co-operation) and NAM (Non-Aligned Movement) summits over the years and steered Bhutan into the comity of nations. Today, the kingdom shares diplomatic ties with 22 countries and more than 30 regional and international organisations, and the international community applauds Bhutan's unique identity and the traditional legacies that it has preserved.

A Monarch of the People

The reign of King Jigme Singye Wangchuck has been described as an epic tale in which a divine king nurtured his country and his people to new levels of well-being. His Majesty travelled around the country throughout the years, personally promoting progressive farming, appropriate technology, improved rural housing, education and health. The kingdom's development planners speak in awe of their king, who read files late into the night, drafted documents and policies, and memorised development statistics in a tireless bid to move Bhutan forward on the path of progress. A UN development adviser once said that the king was the best development consultant she had ever seen at work.

Bhutan's development history shows that, in four decades, the country attained what other countries took centuries to achieve. Life expectancy has jumped from 44 to 66 years of age, and there are now 29 district hospitals and 176 health units. A student population of 146,000 is enrolled in 507 schools and institutions. The road network stretches 4,555 kilometres, and power lines stretch across the vast terrain to provide electricity to more than 1,200 villages.

The reign of King Jigme Singye Wangchuck has been described as an epic tale in which a divine king nurtured his country and his people to new levels of well-being

Above: His Royal Highness the young Crown Prince was a keen sportsman.
Opposite page: A guard of honour for His Royal Highness the Crown Prince.

In the fiscal year 2006-07, Bhutan's GDP had crossed US$1,350 per capita, the highest in South Asia.

"When Druk Gyalpo Jigme Singye Wangchuck was enthroned, a dark night turned into a bright day," says a farmer in remote Zhemgang Valley. "We wore our first shoes, we ate fresh rice from our farms, we turned on electric bulbs at night, we travelled on buses, our children went to school and doctors treated us when we were sick. This was all one man's vision to make his people happy."

His Majesty's journeys around the kingdom are best remembered for his closeness to the people. He knew farmers in remote corners of the kingdom by name. He followed their efforts to double crop paddies and their experiments with new vegetables and cash crops, and he knew their day-to-day problems and concerns. Year after year, His Majesty celebrated National Day and other festivals with the people, joining them in traditional sports and games and sharing their meals.

"This is the real feeling of nationhood," said an old

We wore our first shoes... our children went to school and doctors treated us when we were sick. This was all one man's vision to make his people happy

farmer from Orong village during the 1998 National Day celebrations in Samdrup Jongkhar. "Look at us! From His Majesty the King down to the smallest child, we are eating together, dancing together, playing together and, best of all, laughing together. This is the gathering of the Bhutanese family."

His Majesty gave the people the dignity that he himself epitomised, through the simple life that he led, living in a sparse log cabin among pristine pine forests. An American journalist was surprised to learn that His Majesty believed that a good king needed – more than any grandeur – fairness, honesty and common sense.

But it is His Majesty the fourth Druk Gyalpo's enlightened development philosophy that reverberates around the world today. Gross National Happiness has not only offered a higher goal for development; it has become a reminder to humankind that man must not forget the true purpose of life. GNH, an inspiration that His Majesty offered to the world, states that the quest for material well-being is inadequate. It is more important that people are happy.

His Majesty has become a symbol of the fine balance between modernity and tradition. Based on the pragmatic understanding that Bhutan will never be a military power or an economic force, His Majesty saw the unique Bhutanese identity as the country's fundamental strength. He preserved Bhutan's delicate cultural legacy and ensured that traditional architecture and language, visual and performing arts, and all other aspects of the culture flourished.

"We believe that the roots of a people must be carefully nurtured and the traditional values fostered, so that the trauma of material change does not destroy the cultural identity of a people," he said.

For these and other achievements, His Majesty was voted by the American media, specifically *Time* magazine, as one of the 100 most influential people in the world in 2006. His Majesty was also awarded the 2006 J. Paul Getty Award for Conservation Leadership in recognition of his leadership in establishing a series of policies and laws that have had a positive impact on conservation and environmental sustainability in Bhutan.

Destiny

The Bhutanese people understand that the fourth Druk Gyalpo's vision for Bhutan was planned with a clarity of vision that can only be understood in hindsight. Early during his reign His Majesty said, "The destiny of the nation lies in the hands of the people." The formal process of devolving power to the people began in 1981 when His Majesty established the Dzongkhag Yargye Tshogdue to involve the Bhutanese people in the decision-making process. In 1991, the Geog Yargye Tshogchung was established, further decentralising this process.

After two decades of the 'decentralisation' process, His Majesty decided that the people were ready for more responsibility. In 1998, His Majesty devolved all executive power to a council of elected ministers. A stunned National Assembly pleaded with His Majesty not to give up the reins of governance. "How can we go back to the people and confess that we have allowed such an unimaginable decision?" a member asked.

But that was just the start.

In September 2001, His Majesty commanded the writing of a constitution. Then in December 2005, His Majesty announced in Trashiyangtse that he was stepping down and that Crown Prince Khesar would

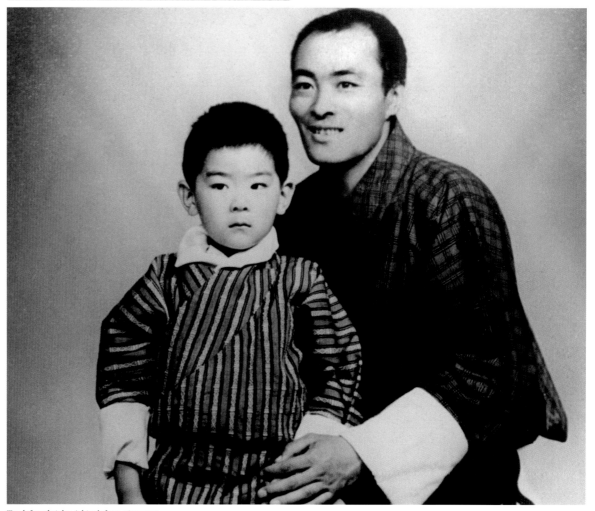

Top left and right: A king's formative years.
Bottom: His Majesty Jigme Dorji Wangchuck and His Royal Highness the Crown Prince.
Opposite page: His Royal Highness the Trongsa Penlop with His Majesty the third Druk Gyalpo, Her Majesty the Queen Mother and the royal family.

His Majesty with Her Majesty the Queen Mother.

Top: His Royal Highness the Crown Prince and their Royal Highnesses the Princesses at boarding school in Darjeeling, India.
Bottom left: A cricketer in a boarding school in England. His Majesty at 10 years of age.
Bottom right: His Royal Highness the Trongsa Penlop in 1972.

be enthroned in 2008. An overwhelmed population responded to such dramatic political developments with disbelief as His Majesty personally began consultations on the contents of the draft Constitution.

The essence of this political legacy lay in two questions: why and why now? The Bhutanese people received answers in His Majesty's own words.

Why? Bhutan is too small and too vulnerable to be left in the hands of one person who is chosen by birth and not by merit. The destiny of the country must, indeed, be left in the hands of the Bhutanese people. Today it is the people who will elect a government and a system that will take Bhutan into the future.

Why now? This is the best time for change. Bhutan is at the peak of the socio-economic development process. The kingdom has never been so secure and stable. Relations with the outside world are at their best, and the friendship and co-operation with India has attained new heights. Change works best during good times.

To a New Era

As both a personification of humility and sensitivity and a leader who has genuine affection for his people, many Bhutanese believe that His Majesty the fourth Druk Gyalpo is a manifestation of Chenrezig, the Lord of Compassion. The greatest lesson that His Majesty leaves for the Bhutanese people to ponder is the powerful Buddhist teaching of impermanence.

The dignity of His Majesty could not have been better expressed than through his quiet detachment from worldly power. Having won the hearts of the people as the king, His Majesty completely overwhelmed them by giving up the throne. When King Jigme Singye Wangchuck stepped down, he did so as a man who had reached his destiny.

The dramatic political transformation in Bhutan today is understood as a royal gesture of faith and trust in the Bhutanese people. During his coronation speech on June 2, 1974, His Majesty told the people: "As for you, my people, are concerned, you should not adopt the attitude that whatever is required to be done for your welfare will be done entirely by the government. On the contrary, a little effort on your part will be more effective than a great deal of effort on the part of the government."

This message rings true today as the Kingdom of Bhutan welcomes a new king, a new legend, a new era.

Three days of celebrations followed the investiture of the Trongsa Penlop in May 1972.
His Royal Highness the Crown Prince joins officials from the government in a tug of war.

Photo: left and right: © Rajesh Bedi

His Royal Highness the Trongsa Penlop with Khyentse Rinpoche at Dechenchholing Palace on March 15, 1972.
His Royal Highness the Crown Prince had earlier that day received the ceremonial scarves that signify his rank as the Trongsa Penlop at Tashichhodzong.

The royal wedding. His Majesty the fourth Druk Gyalpo with (right to left) Her Majesty Ashi Sangay Choden Wangchuck,
Her Majesty Ashi Dorji Wangmo Wangchuck, Her Majesty Ashi Tshering Pem Wangchuck and Her Majesty Ashi Tshering Yangdon Wangchuck.

His Royal Highness the Trongsa Penlop inspects the troops.

If the government and the people join hands and work with determination, our people will achieve prosperity and our nation will become strong and stable...the only message that I have to convey to you today, my people, is that if every one of us consider ourselves Bhutanese and think and act as one, and if we have faith in the Triple Gem, our glorious Kingdom of Bhutan will grow from strength to strength and achieve prosperity, peace and happiness.

His Majesty Jigme Singye Wangchuck
June 3, 1974

His Majesty the King with (from right to left) H.R.H. the Crown Prince Dasho Jigme Khesar Namgyel Wangchuck, H.R.H. Dasho Jigyel Ugyen Wangchuck, H.R.H. Dasho Khasum Singye Wangchuck and H.R.H. Dasho Jigme Dorji Wangchuck. Opposite page: His Majesty the fourth Druk Gyalpo addresses the nation the day after his coronation at Changlimithang stadium.

Unlike bigger countries, we do not have military might or economic strength, but we have a rich cultural heritage and a unique national identity to enhance our status as a sovereign, independent country.

His Majesty Jigme Singye Wangchuck

Chapter Two

A Century of Monarchy

རྒྱལ་པོའི་བསྟན་བཤུགས།། National Anthem

འབྲུག་ཙན་དན་བཀོད་པའི་རྒྱལ་ཁབ་ན།། In the Thunder Dragon Kingdom where cypresses grow

དཔལ་ལུགས་གཉིས་བསྟན་སྲིད་སྐྱོང་བའི་མགོན།། A refuge of the glorious monastic and civil traditions

འབྲུག་རྒྱལ་པོ་མངའ་བདག་རིན་པོ་ཆེ།། The King of Druk Yul, precious sovereign

སྐུ་འགྱུར་མེད་བརྟན་ཅིང་ཆབ་སྲིད་འཕེལ།། His being is eternal, his reign prosperous

ཆོས་སངས་རྒྱས་བསྟན་པ་དར་ཞིང་རྒྱས།། The teachings of enlightenment thrive and flourish

འབངས་བདེ་སྐྱིད་ཉི་མ་ཤར་བར་ཤོག།། May the sun of peace and happiness shine on all the people

His Majesty King Ugyen Wangchuck

Reign: 1907-1926

His Majesty King Jigme Wangchuck

Reign: 1926-1952

The year 2008 marks the centenary of the Bhutanese Monarchy under the Wangchuck dynasty. The Kings of Bhutan have taken the country and its people into the 21st Century, transforming a subsistence farming society into a modern nation. The Bhutanese people are now on the path to democracy, a revolutionary move initiated from the throne. But the monarchy remains the soul of the Bhutanese nation and will continue to be a vital institution in a rapidly changing society.

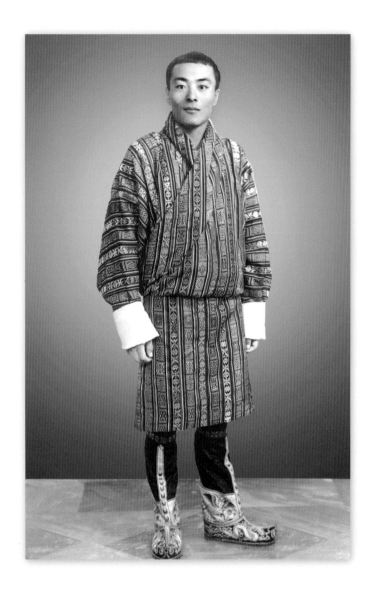

His Majesty Jigme Dorji Wangchuck

Reign: 1952–1972

His Majesty Jigme Singye Wangchuck

Reign: 1972–2006

His Majesty Jigme Dorji Wangchuck and His Royal Highness the Crown Prince during the Army Sports Week in 1971.

His Majesty Jigme Khesar Namgyel Wangchuck

Reign: 2006 – present

Above: His Majesty Jigme Khesar Namgyel Wangchuck addresses the country on National Day, 2006.
Opposite page: His Majesty was crowned the fourth Druk Gyalpo in the fourth month of the Wood Tiger Year, June 2, 1974.

I have always made it clear that the people are more important than the King. We cannot leave the future of the country in the hands of one person who is chosen by birth and not by merit.

His Majesty Jigme Singye Wangchuck

Chapter Three

A People's Tribute

Photo: left Kiattipong Panchee · right Polleur

ཕྱོགས་ལས་རྣམ་པར་རྒྱལ་བའི་གླུ་དབྱངས།

A Song of Victory

Outwardly He is the conqueror of negative forces,
Inwardly He is Padma Sambhava, the protector,
Secretly He is Avalokitesvara, the source of compassion.
He is a ruler with the name 'Jigme'
Who attained victory in all the directions
And kept the banner of fame flying in the sky.

When Heruka, the glorious supreme steed,
Destroyed Matram Rudra, the original ego-demon
In Malaya, the summit of the volcanic mountain,
The wrathful deity roared with laughter.

Under the Bodhi tree at Bodh Gaya,
Shakyamuni conquered the four negative forces,
And spread the melody of eighty-four thousand
Dharma teachings in all the three realms.

At the thirty-third heaven, the realm of gods,
Indra, the lord of the gods,
Sang a song of victory, of good prevailing over evil,
After gaining victory over the demi-gods.

Likewise, in the country of medicinal herbs,
I sang a song of happiness
After the religious king, Jigme Singye,
Defeated the enemy of Buddha dharma completely.
If one does not know what song it is,
It is the song of victory in all the directions,
It is the song of sublime aspirations and prosperity.
Please listen a while to such a song.

In the state of Kham in ancient times,
Just as the powerful king Gesar
Came north to the land of the maras (negative forces),
King Jigme Singye too came
From the land of the glorious Pelden Drukpa,
palace of Avalokitesvara.
He headed towards the southern region,
According to the prophecy of the dakinis,
In the Female Water Sheep Year,
The beginning of the tenth lunar month.

Many were left behind at the time,
Including mothers, sons, queens, ministers and subjects,
Just as a child separated from the mother,
Wandered in the darkness of worrisome plains.

It is true that one cannot bear the pain of separation.
If we think with illusion without deliberating
We feel like crying our eyes out,
Out of love, compassion and affectionate feelings.
But having deliberated very carefully,
I have concluded with this thought:
That He is not a common person.

Commissioned from the pure castle of gods,
For the sake of sentient beings,
That He will not protect us is inconceivable.
That is why He is an emanated king.

There is Ugyen Pema on the top,
There is heroic Zhabdrung at the back,
There is raven on the right,
There is Mahakali on the left,
There are blue and red protectors in the front.
May the clouds of blessings encircle
From the lineage teachers on the top.
May the rains of accomplishments
Fall from the dakinis in the centre.
May the deeds appear like the flash of lightning
From the eight associates of dharma protector from below.

I think there is no need to panic
Because there is a state of mental peace.
But, there should be prayers and bringing together of
auspicious thoughts and actions,
And there should be sincere commitment.
There should also be combined merits of the people.
When the evil deeds of the people increase,
Even the powers of the thousand Buddhas are destroyed.

All the virtuous religious rites
Have been performed as intended
To accumulate merits for us and for others
Though it was not necessary for the religious king.
The life of the religious king is safe,
The sovereignty of the country is protected,
The obstacle to the teachings of Buddhism is cleared,
The minds of people are united than ever,
Brothers and sisters with identical commitments!
Let us express our gratitude and appreciation!
Thus far it is the song of auspiciousness.

The rebellious insurgents of the three Indian militant groups,
Possessing courage like that of wild carnivores,
Wandered in the thick jungles and trench-valleys,
With dreaded arms and ammunitions
Piled up like heaps of grains in the storehouse.
Obsessed with the thought of challenging
The government of the mighty republic of India,
They established military camps on hills and in valleys
On the edges between the east and the west.

The evil insurgents laid their destructive hands and legs
On the holy land of medicinal herbs.
Although Bhutan initiated many peace talks in six years,
They tried to challenge us instead of relinquishing.

There were rumors in India
That even if a minimum of ten soldiers
Fought with a single militant,
It would not have been possible to win.

But, with the steadfast determination of His Majesty,
The brave and courageous armed forces,
Who always worship the Buddha, Dharma and Sangha,
Who take the command of His Majesty in their hearts,
Inspired by the great patriotism for one's own country,
Risked life and limb to defend the country.

As soon as they arrived at the militant camps,
They removed the insurgents in one fell swoop,
As if a conch shell perforates a whale,
Because of the inevitable truth of causality.

Just as a cliff collapses as if struck by lightning,
The 30 camps set up
Were turned to ashes and blown off by the air,
Within a time span of just one day.

It is a pity that they tried to destroy us.
However, it is not proper to despise them,
As they are also members of sentient beings.
So, we performed many virtuous acts for their cause.

We offered prayers for them to attain enlightenment.
May you guide them through the path
To Sukhavati, the paradise of Avalokitesvara!
Om Mani Padme Hum!

The sun of expected result has shone,
The darkness of doubt has been cleared,
How great and wonderful it is,
How happy and peaceful it is,
May the Triple Gem always prevail!
May Palden Drukpa, the glorious Bhutan, always prevail!
The sons of Palden Drukpa
Have fought many wars, but never have been vanquished.
This indicates that there is something great in us,
Our inner values, the law of causality, are always maintained.
Thus far it is the song of victory over the enemies.

From here, it is the expression of good fortune.
Good fortune to His Majesty, the religious king,
Who is the sovereign of the two systems.
Good fortune to the gracious queens,
Who are the dakinis and companions.
Good fortune to the competent ministers,
Who possess great skills of governance.
Good fortune to the war commander,
Who is the hero and the courageous war-god.
Good fortune to the faithful subjects,
Who follow the commands with loyalty and dedication.
Good fortune to the Buddha, Dharma and Sangha,
Who are the infallible sources of prayer and blessing.
We offer this song to the deities and protectors,
May all the enemies be suppressed by their powers!
We offer this song to 'lamas, the supreme teachers',
May you lead through the path of liberation!
We offer this song to the powerful ruler,
May you conquer all the three realms!
We offer this song to the assemblage of goddesses,
May there be peace and happiness,
May the king, ministers and all the subjects
Live long lives without any sickness,
May there be peace and prosperity,
May we meet again and again
May we meet together in the pure land,
The heaven of Buddha Amitabha, in the next lives.
May the teachings of Buddhism,
The source of peace and happiness, flourish.

Written by His Holiness the Je Khenpo
Trulku Jigme Choeda 2003
Translation: the Dzongkha Development Authority and Dasho Sangay Wangchug

His Majesty with His Holiness the Je Khenpo (right) and the Je Kudrey Nyizur Trulku (left) during the Silver Jubilee celebrations in 1999.

A Visionary King

His Majesty the fourth Druk Gyalpo takes part in the Tikka ceremony.

Seventy-three-year-old Tulsi Ram Bhandari teaches at one of Bhutan's two Sanskrit institutes in Sarpang Dzongkhag. He first met His Majesty the King in 1988. Over the years, the pandit has been in the presence of the fourth Druk Gyalpo more than 15 times, mostly during the Durga Puja ceremony at the Samteling Royal Cottage in Thimphu.

"His Majesty the fourth Druk Gyalpo is a true incarnation of Lord Vishnu and has served the Buddha dharma and his people from a very early age," says Pandit Tulsi Ram Bhandari. "Through His Majesty's far-sighted vision and the blessings of the Lord Buddha, Bhutan has remained a sovereign country."

"His Majesty provided special monetary subsidies to the two Sanskrit institutes of learning: the Pathshalas in Surey and Dobhan in Sarpang," he says. "The people of Sarpang are ever grateful for the support. We, the pandit and purohit (lay priests) of Surey and Dochan, were deeply privileged when His Majesty the King put tikka on our foreheads with his own hands."

"His Majesty has provided free education for Bhutanese children, free medical services for the people, and built roads and bridges that have helped generate rural income," says Tulsi Ram Bhandari. "The fourth Druk Gyalpo's emphasis on Bhutan's environment and preservation of its tradition and culture are, today, a symbol of Bhutan's unique identity."

"His Majesty has been guiding people on the right path. We pray for the long life and good health of His Majesty the fourth Druk Gyalpo, His Majesty the King and the royal family."

Pandit Tulsi Ram Bhandari
Teacher
Laxmi Narayan Mandir, Surey

A Golden Era and a Fairytale King

His Majesty on the archery pitch.

Photo: left © Kuensel Corporation • right courtesy Lyonpo Sangay Ngedup

I f you look into the history of Bhutan, it has been one of the most progressive countries. Every change that led us to the 21st Century has come from the top down, never from the bottom up. We gave up the feudal system and set up the national assembly system. We had to train people to share power. This is all a part of getting people ready for democracy. His Majesty has been preparing us for this.

His Majesty is a man of wisdom and, as far as I know, he never believed in the rule of one man. His Majesty has never been a person to make frivolous decisions. Every move, every decision of his, has been well thought out, balanced and in the interest of the country.

His Majesty is a great person for consultations, knowing what people want. He's always gone through a tremendous process of consultation with the public from the very beginning, getting to know his people at the grassroots level, and he is a

tremendous judge of character. Not only is he King, he is a human being. That's the most important aspect of this king of ours. He is a human being who feels very strongly…who cares.

Here lies his greatness. He could have had tremendous power, but by giving it away, he has become a greater man. He's almost become a demi-god, as far as I'm concerned.

This country has been so lucky to have this lineage of kings. Looking back at 34 years of His Majesty's reign, it's been a golden era with a fairytale king. His Majesty the fourth Druk Gyalpo is a hard act to follow and almost impossible to surpass.

Dasho Paljor J. Dorji
Former Chief Justice

Meeting my King

Tashi meets His Majesty the fourth Druk Gyalpo.

Tashi is all smiles whenever he recalls the moment when he first met His Majesty the fourth Druk Gyalpo. It was in 1997 in Sarpang, and he was six years old. He was a kindergarten student at the primary school.

That morning his father had told him that His Majesty the King was visiting the school. With great excitement, Tashi put on his uniform and walked happily to school thinking all the way about his king, whose portrait hangs on a wall at home. "I used to ask my parents about His Majesty and they told me that he is a great king."

He remembers a flurry of activity as many cars drove into the compound. The students were fidgeting with excitement. Tashi, who was standing in front, tried not to turn around to look at the royal entourage. A tall, kind looking man strode to the front of the school assembly, which was being held outside in the warmth of the morning. He sat down on the steps in front of the school. He took a look around and

suddenly beckoned to Tashi to come forward.

The next few minutes were like a dream. "I didn't know if I was scared, or excited, or proud. I only know he was a gentle, kind person, like a caring father," recalls Tashi as he looks at the now familiar picture of His Majesty talking to him a decade ago. His Majesty talked to him about his family and told him to go and play with Their Royal Highnesses.

Since then Tashi's friends often gather around him, asking him to recount the conversation over and over again. It is still a dream.

Tashi Palden Dorji
16-year-old student
Paro

Photo: left courtesy Lyonpo Sangay Ngedup • right © Chencho Norbu

His Majesty the fourth Druk Gyalpo, Their Majesties the Queens, H.R.H. Ashi Chimi Yangzom Wangchuck and H.R.H. Ashi Sonam Dechan Wangchuck.

How Can a King Retire?

His Majesty at an agricultural programme showcasing new technology.

The fourth Druk Gyalpo's retirement shocked the Bhutanese. "We have never heard of such a thing. How can a king retire? What kind of a foreign idea is this?" asks 74-year-old Agay Dago from Paro. "He is the sun in our lives… what we eat, what we wear, we owe to him."

Agay said he and his family felt very hurt when His Majesty announced through the draft Constitution that the Druk Gyalpo must retire at the age of 65 years. "We begged him, saying that if this was an international idea that we simple people did not understand, then he should retire at 70 or 75 years."

"Then His Majesty announced in Trashiyangtse that he would retire in 2008. We had grave doubts and fears. And in 2006 he stepped down from the throne."

"But now, how can we complain when he left his own prince to rule? We can only expect that our new king will achieve as much if not more than his forefathers."

Agay Dago
Silversmith
Paro

His Majesty Jigme Singye Wangchuck: An Epic King

His Majesty the fourth Druk Gyalpo.

Photo: left © Nado • right courtesy Lyonpo Sangay Ngedup

Bhutan has been, and I feel it will always be, blessed with selfless rulers who put the country before self. Having said that, I think the fourth King, His Majesty Jigme Singye Wangchuck, will always stand apart. What Shabdrung Ngawang Namgyel initiated 400 years ago, the fourth Druk Gyalpo consolidated and strengthened in order to ensure that this unique little kingdom would continue to exist and thrive not only in the 21st Century, but for all time to come.

Monarchs like His Majesty Jigme Singye Wangchuck are a rarity. He always maintained that monarchy was perhaps not the right form of governance, and in hindsight, we realise that the fourth Druk Gyalpo already had his master plan for Bhutan by the tender age of 17 when he took over the governance of the kingdom.

He single-mindedly strove to fit together Bhutan's democracy jigsaw, piece by piece, over his 34-year reign. Right from the start, His Majesty worked untiringly to empower the people; he placed them centre stage, meeting all the people in the 20 dzongkhags and consulting them on the five-year development plans. The gradual devolution of power with the establishment of the Dzongkhag and the Geog Yargye Tshogchung and the setting up of the Council of Ministers has finally culminated with the introduction of parliamentary democracy in 2008.

The legacies of this wise, dynamic, far-sighted and visionary monarch also include the new development philosophy GNH, Gross National Happiness, environmental conservation and the preservation of Bhutan's unique cultural heritage.

In addition to being a great statesman and general, the fourth Druk Gyalpo, His Majesty Jigme Singye Wangchuck, is a true patriot who has always put the country before all else. He has always lived a simple life. I have never known His Majesty to take a holiday outside the country, nor have I ever seen His Majesty live a lavish lifestyle. His Majesty displays an innate sense of simplicity – from food to clothes to many other activities that surround him.

The fourth Druk Gyalpo is also very thoughtful and sensitive to the needs of those around him. I will always remember how deeply touched I was by this quality in our King. It was in the 1970s, when His Majesty took a whole group of young officers, including myself, on a mountain trek. We had walked the whole day and it was wet and the whole place was covered in snow. We were thirsty and hungry. Provisions were low and an attendant offered an orange to His Majesty – one of few remaining.

His Majesty asked for all the fruit, peeled and then distributed the oranges equally among all those accompanying him. I was really moved by this display of human sensitivity. I know that, over the years, all who have come in touch with the fourth King have witnessed this compassion and sensitivity and been struck by these qualities.

His Majesty King Jigme Singye Wangchuck is my inspiration and, to me, the greatest man that the world has seen. I would say that perhaps Bhutan is too small for the greatness of our King, the fourth Druk Gyalpo, and for the legacy he has left behind. We see the same traits in the fifth King, Druk Gyalpo Jigme Khesar Namgyel Wangchuck, and I am confident that His Majesty will lead Bhutan to even greater heights.

Lyonpo Sangay Ngedup
Former Prime Minister and Cabinet Minister

His Majesty shares a meal with his people after a district meeting.

The True Son of a Lion

His Majesty the fourth Druk Gyalpo with lay monks.

Photo: left and right courtesy Lyonpo Sangay Ngedup

Lopen Pemala, an 83-year-old historian and scholar, remembers when His Majesty delivered his first speech to the National Assembly at the age of 16, "We came away surprised and deeply moved by his words. Here was a true leader. His Majesty showed himself to be the true son of a lion."

Lopen Pemala, now in permanent Buddhist practice, describes His Majesty Jigme Singye Wangchuck as a monarch who embraces religion and all that is good (Choe len) to benefit everyone. "His Majesty has demonstrated that he thinks and lives only for the benefit of the people, and because of that, His Majesty has an auspicious and strong aura that has helped to dispel ill fortune from Bhutan. Because of these good deeds, His Majesty will live happily."

Lopen Pemala believes that the fourth Druk Gyalpo has a natural inner aptitude for spirituality and has been identified by great dharma teachers like Dilgo

Khyentse Rinpoche as a Bodhisattva. "His Majesty's initiatives show his dedication to the spiritual path. In the past, monks had to go around begging for food; His Majesty has given the monk body security and allowed spiritual practice to flourish. He has been responsible for the establishment of the shedras and drubdras, and the support has enabled so many people to practise Buddhism and to generate well-being."

On the process of democratisation that the fourth Druk Gyalpo has initiated, Lopen Pemala says, "We know that the fourth Druk Gyalpo thinks only of the welfare and benefit of our people. If your thoughts are good, then the place and the path you take can only be good."

Lopen Pemala
Retired
Nimalung Monastery, Bumthang

Our Most Trusted Parent

His Majesty the fourth Druk Gyalpo and His Holiness the Je Khenpo.

Ugyen, a retired chimi says, "The fourth Druk Gyalpo has improved the people's livelihood, brought economic progress, political reform and even risked his own life for the security of Bhutan. He is a true heart son of the people and our most trusted parent. We were filled with sorrow on hearing the news that our fourth Druk Gyalpo is retiring from the golden throne."

Seventy-year-old Ugyen's biggest regret in life is the fact that he was not able to express thanks and gratitude to His Majesty the fourth Druk Gyalpo at the eighty-fifth session of the National Assembly.

Representing Khatoe and Khame geogs in Gasa, Ugyen met His Majesty the fourth Druk Gyalpo during development plan meetings in Punakha when Gasa was still a dungkhag, "His Majesty was the king of the country, but he is spiritually no other than the manifestation of Guru Rinpoche."

Ugyen
Retired chimi
Gasa

A Period of Bliss

The King and his people: A period of bliss.

Seventy-eight-year-old Ap Pangla believes that the reign of the fourth Druk Gyalpo was "a period of bliss". "When he came it was like dawn breaking. We started crossing rivers that we didn't cross before and climbing mountains that we couldn't climb," says Ap Pangla, a government clerk in the 1960s. "Who could have dreamt that people would be travelling through the sky?"

"We hear of people around the world dying of starvation, being washed away by floods, of falling victim to so many diseases. Here, even in the most remote of places, we are enjoying peace and tranquillity. It can't get better."

This is all because of the vision and efforts of one man.

And this is also the reason that the retired civil servant is concerned about the changes taking place today. "In placing the destiny of the country in the hands of the people, His Majesty means well for us, but common people do not have the vision

of kings. Kings can reach where we cannot reach; they can see things that we cannot see," says Ap Pangla, who now lives in retirement in remote Zhemgang.

"His Majesty has given us a constitution, but can we implement it? I fear that it might be like giving a turnip to a monkey. Giving the wrong people power might not benefit the country. I say this because, even before democracy has started, we see problems here in the rural areas."

"That is why His Majesty the King must continue to guide us. We do not want to leave behind the tranquillity that we are enjoying."

Ap Pangla
Retired
Zhemgang

The Courage to Act

His Majesty the fourth Druk Gyalpo and a local leader at a district meeting.

I served His Majesty the fourth King for 10 years on his personal staff, and it was a most wonderful experience.

One of the most striking qualities of the fourth Druk Gyalpo is his kindness. He would always look into the welfare of all his staff…whether we were eating well, that we were not exposed to the cold…he would give us blankets when we travelled at night. This was a human quality I have not seen in people at that level. It meant that, while His Majesty's wisdom soared high above, he had his feet planted on the ground.

His vision for Bhutan was drawn from his kindness and concern for the common people. In fact, His Majesty never had personal interests. There are many people in the world who are kind and great in thought and word, but do not inspire or produce action.

Time will tell that the sterling quality of His Majesty is his courage, courage to act and implement his wisdom. No common mortal could have done that. One of them is the drafting of the Constitution. The nation didn't want it, people didn't want it, but he felt it was necessary. He lived by his word and history will elaborate on that.

The whole world was sailing through a period of westernisation that was interpreted as progress. His Majesty thought otherwise, and, here again, it was His Majesty's wisdom that enabled Bhutan to strike the balance between culture, tradition, religion and development – a symbiotic process that has helped the nation progress.

His Majesty was never arrogant. Many times, ministers and civil servants would submit: "You are a king, Your Majesty should not receive this person." But His Majesty showed the example that national interest is supreme and not subservient to personal ego.

Right from the beginning, His Majesty talked about the environment and decentralisation. Some of the ministers then said, "There is so much forest; why do we need to be environmentally conscious?" But we understand His Majesty's wisdom and realise now how ignorant and wrong we were.

His Majesty strengthened the sense of nationhood and national identity by celebrating National Day in remote dzongkhags. Everybody wore the national dress and kabneys, ate Bhutanese food, and played traditional games and sports. It played a very important role. The people were able to meet their King. His Majesty took part in the games and served the people. When His Majesty served drinks, people drank, because to receive from his hand is so sacred that it will cleanse defilements.

As recently as the 1980s, Bhutan was not known or respected. His Majesty transformed this nation. When we used to say we're Bhutanese, people asked where is Bhutan? Now we are a nation that can hold its head high; we can talk to other countries. We are playing an important role in the international arena. Today, we are proud to say we're Bhutanese wherever we go.

By abdicating, His Majesty taught us the real lesson of impermanence and showed us the strength needed to devolve power and authority in time.

Generally, leadership does not develop under a very strong leader. But His Majesty trained leaders, and we now have leaders to carry on the work that he started. This is one of His Majesty's great contributions. Democracy is injected in the people so that more people will participate under a credible leadership and a fair system. His Majesty has always said that "good governance is central to a successful democracy."

Lyonpo Sonam Tobgye
Chief Justice

A Bhutanese voter at mock elections in April 2007.

A Tribute

National Day celebrations in Samtse in 2002.

I had the great honour and privilege of serving His Majesty since his days at school in North Point, Darjeeling in the early 1960s, until he became the Crown Prince in 1972 at the tender age of sixteen.

Hence, I take pride in saying that I have served His Majesty for a lifetime.

I stood in great awe of our King. His concern for the people from all parts of the country, his compassionate vision and drive to improve people's welfare, well-being and livelihoods are most admirable. The King respected all religions and especially Buddhism and Hinduism. He always wanted to do what was right and not what was simply popular. I sincerely believe that had it not been for the direct intervention of His Majesty in the early 1970s, the national Monk Body would not have been what it

is today, the environment and forests of Bhutan may have been damaged seriously, and the national foreign exchange reserves and the exchequer may have been frittered away. He was deeply concerned with children's education and would go to great lengths to ensure the health and well-being of the people, even if medical treatment had to be obtained at great expense to the government.

My family and I will always fondly and respectfully cherish the personal consideration shown to us throughout our lives by His Majesty King Jigme Singye Wangchuck, the fourth Druk Gyalpo and Their Majesties the Queens.

Lyonpo Om Pradhan
Former Minister

The Blessings of Chenrezig

Aum Kinley's meeting with His Majesty the King during a district meeting in 1997.

Aum Kinley Tshering has been blessed. She says that the personification of Chenrezig has touched her. It was in 1997 that the former tshogpa stood near His Majesty the King during the dzonkhag's Seventh Plan meeting.

"Because of His Majesty we now have roads. For those without electricity, His Majesty has provided electricity. We can now talk to our children on the telephone even if they are far away. His Majesty has given us a much better life," says Aum Kinley.

Like many people of her generation, Aum Kinley regards His Majesty as the manifestation of Chenrezig. He is the sun of happiness that has enabled every-one to live harmoniously. Aum Kinley treasures the kira and toeko she wore that day. "I am keeping this as my sungma, and I will bequeath it to my grandchildren so they too will be blessed." She remembers being plagued by regular illnesses all her life. She has not been sick since that day. Thinking about that moment, she begins chanting: "May our fourth Druk Gyalpo live long. May the Bhutanese people live happily. May our fifth Druk Gyalpo reign successfully like his father."

Aum Kinley Tshering
Paro
Shaba

Monarchy, the Soul of Bhutan

Monarchy and spirituality: the essence of Bhutan.

The development of Bhutan in the last 34 years is something that is almost unimaginable for most people. We're still a developing country, but Bhutan was a different place 30 years ago. Thimphu was like a village – there were no proper roads, everything was dusty and dirty, there was no sanitation, no proper health facilities. One can only imagine what the rest of the country was like.

When His Majesty took over I was still in college. Being relatively well-educated, some of us were more worried about Bhutan than others. It was a country at this very early stage of development, with a very young boy at the helm of things who had no experience. We were also at a stage where a King was not supported by a competent bureaucracy. We had a few deputationists from India who helped with development activities, but, by and large, the King relied on a few old ministers.

His Majesty, in spite of his very young age, demonstrated a tremendous amount of maturity and common sense as soon as he took over. It was amazing. I came up to Bhutan in 1973, and His Majesty told me to work with him, so I stayed with His Majesty's gokha (court). The fourth Druk Gyalpo had a tremendous sense of maturity.

He was in the process of finding his own way around, but he did it very wisely. His Majesty did not have an ego as a King; he was willing to listen to young people, old people, anybody.

There were groups of people being called to the palace every now and then, where in a very informal setting, he would probe their thoughts. His Majesty would talk about all sorts of activities, and he was so good that these interactions became like brainstorming sessions from which the King learned a lot about the government itself. He was running the government for the first time, so these things enabled him to understand the situation in Bhutan far better.

In the early days of kingship, Kings are usually aloof from everybody else, but the fourth Druk Gyalpo was able to understand because he interacted very intensely with people.

His Majesty had that inborn natural quality of leadership and a tremendous amount of wisdom. He could break a problem down, step by step, and had the ability to see a total picture very quickly. Most of the time people see things in bits and pieces and get very excited, but he was able to see the total picture very quickly, and that is a great quality of the King.

Initially, most of the activities focused on institution building. When we first started development, we built roads, then schools, then hospitals. We didn't go into any fancy projects. We went into what was basic and necessary, and I think that really helped to sustain a lot of things. The greatest achievement is that, having brought the country this far, His Majesty is introducing democracy. He did everything that needed to be done, slowly but surely and not overnight: development, sovereignty, national security and then handing over his own power to the people of Bhutan.

His Majesty first started talking about Gross National Happiness in the early 1980s. We had started talking about the need to do many things and much about self-reliance. We were so dependent on donors at the time, but I remember His Majesty saying that we should not have illusions of development. It's good to think about things, but we can't do everything at the same time with the limited resources and limited capacity that we have. We must move in the right path, and the most important thing to remember is that the people of Bhutan should be happy.

The fourth Druk Gyalpo is a wonderful human being; you feel so much peace around him. Monarchy is the soul of Bhutan. This country cannot do without monarchy.

Lyonpo Yeshey Zimba
Former Prime Minister and Cabinet Minister

A King and his people during National Day celebrations in Trashiyangtse, 2005.

Meeting his people. His Majesty the fourth Druk Gyalpo during the Silver Jubilee celebrations in Thimphu in 1999.

His Majesty playing soksum at National Day celebrations in Trashiyangtse, 2005.

His Majesty the fourth Druk Gyalpo at the National Assembly in 1994.

Bhutan's National Assembly meets in the presence of His Majesty the King of Bhutan.

The Constitution must ensure the well-being of the country, serve the needs of the people and fulfil their aspirations. Bhutan is extremely fortunate today, because we have the time and the opportunity to achieve this cherished goal.

His Majesty Jigme Singye Wangchuck

Chapter Four

In The News

The Indian Express   June 2, 1974

King of Bhutan Crowned in all Splendour

By A.N. Dar in Thimphu

Medieval times mingled with the twentieth century at the crowning here this morning of His Majesty Jigme Singye Wangchuck as the King of Bhutan.

The Presidents of India and Bangladesh, the Chogyal of Sikkim and diplomatic representatives of 12 countries as far removed as the United States and China were present in the gilded throne room of the historic Tashichhodzong Castle where the two-hour coronation ceremony for the world's youngest monarch took place.

One had to be here to believe that so much colour and pageantry is possible in real life and not just in a technicolour film. It was a feast of beauty, rich colours and high religious rites all magically woven together in a ceremony called coronation. It left the people enthralled.

At the auspicious hour of 9:10 am, King Jigme Singye Wangchuck, 'the fearless lion born of lightning', was offered the five coloured scarves of Bhutanese Kings by the Je Khenpo, the head of all lamas in Bhutan. This, falling on the thirteenth day of the fourth month of the Bhutanese Wood Tiger Year, was the crowning moment of the three-day celebrations which began today. The wearing of the Royal Crown with the raven head on top is not necessary at the coronation.

It was hoary medieval splendour at its colourful best. It was also intensely modern in many ways. The 5-km procession of the King, which meandered through the mountains from his palace to Tashichhodzong, was led by a white horse wearing a silken scarf symbolising purity. In the middle was a caparisoned elephant, a present from the people of Southern Bhutan. The King himself came in a glittering blue Ford towards the end of the procession, which included, on foot, his ministers, legislators, students, prominent lamas and people dancing their way towards Tashichhodzong.

Thirty senior lamas stood on top of Tashichhodzong blowing trumpets and horns and beating drums and cymbals as the King down below inspected a smart Guard of Honour formed by the Royal Guards who carried semi-automatic rifles with bayonets blazing in the Himalayan sun.

As the 31 guns were fired in salute to the King the mountains echoed and re echoed the boom through the Thimphu valley, and the smoke mixed with patches of clouds here and there. In this fantastic setting the coronation ceremonies slowly started.

The bachelor King, with his 18 years sitting calmly on his handsome features, went through the ceremonies with the calm and serenity that could only be expected from a child of the Himalayas. Nearby was the Queen Grandmother, a picture of age and wisdom. The Queen Mother sitting next to her was a blaze of colour in her tier upon tier of rich brocade. The King's bevy of three sisters, who are amongst his closest advisors in the administration, looked on as beautifully as is to be expected in a country where roses are found in profusion and precious orchids grow wild.

With this final ceremony to herald his kingship, King Jigme Singye Wangchuck became the fourth hereditary monarch of this 18,000-sq mile kingdom of 1.1 million people that stands between two great Asian countries, India and China.

The Wangchuck dynasty started in 1907, when the religious and administrative authorities were combined into one person. But the rituals of the coronation, which we witnessed today, reach back into seemingly ageless Bhutanese history. The ceremonies over, the representatives of various countries offered gifts to the King. Mr. V.V. Giri was the first to do so. The countries represented by their diplomats were Canada, China, the Soviet Union, the USA, Nepal, New Zealand, Australia, Britain, Japan and France. Representatives had also been invited from Burma and Sri Lanka, but they were not present at the ceremony today.

It was truly a great day for Bhutan. Since early morning, when the mist started clearing from the peaks and the overnight rain stopped, all mountain roads, bridle paths and river banks led to Tashichhodzong. As a select gathering filled the courtyards of Tashichhodzong, it became an amphitheatre of colour and sound.

Facing a huge image of Guru Padma Sambhava, the monk from Nalanda who brought Buddhism to Bhutan, the King touched the national flag, whose yellow half symbolises his secular authority and orange half, his religious practice. The snarling mouth of the dragon on the flag expresses the stern strength of the deities which are supposed to protect Bhutan

Opposite page: The welcoming party for the coronation of the fourth Druk Gyalpo on June 2, 1974

The Hindu   June 3, 1974

Bhutan King Enthroned: Colourful Function at Thimphu

By K. Krishna Moorthy

King Jigme Singye Wangchuck was enthroned this morning as the monarch of Bhutan, at a ceremony at the Royal Fort Palace here to the accompaniment of elaborate and colourful religious and social rituals whose origins are lost in legends and history.

The 18-year-old King received the multi-coloured traditional scarf of Royal Office from the Je Khenpo, the Chief and Incarnate Lama of Bhutan at an auspicious hour chosen by astrologers shortly after 9am.

The President Mr. V.V. Giri, the President of Bangladesh Mr. Mohammadullah and the Chogyal of Sikkim, who is also related to the Bhutanese Royal family, were the three Heads of State to honour the occasion by their presence, while Nepal sent as its representative Prince Gyanendra.

All the permanent members of the Security Council, including China, sent their Ambassadors or Charge d'Affaires, marking international recognition of the young King's ascension to the throne. The presentation of the scarf by the High Priest to the King was private and secret, unwitnessed and unphotographed. In the small confines of the throne room the King sat without a crown, but wore a highly decorative silken woven dress and ceremonial scarf. Before entering the private chambers for the ceremony, there were some interesting rituals in the courtyard of Tashichhodzong, the Royal Fort Palace, which also includes part of the Secretariat and a huge wing for Buddhist monks.

White Horse Leads Procession

The coronation procession was headed by a white horse which used to symbolise the authority of ancient Hindu Kings. But the ashwa (horse) in Bhutan, officials said, stood for purity of purpose.

A caparisoned elephant also formed part of the procession, which included dancers, musicians, ministers, monks, people's representatives and soldiers. The team of soldiers carried ancient swords and shields and peasants singing folk songs wore hats made out of leaves strung into ropes. Some other participants were decorated with multi-coloured head bands.

A 50-foot high thangka (religious appliqué) hung from the towering top storeys of the palace, facing the raised platform where the King awaited with the High Priest for initiation ceremonies before actually being enthroned inside the palace.

Before and after the initiation ceremonies, hosts of dancers and musicians entertained the distinguished assemblage. Some musicians stood up on the 50-foot-high walls of the Fort Palace blowing extremely long horns, and on the ground, other musicians played on wind instruments and pipes which sounded almost like the North Indian Shehnai.

Scarves Presented

PTI reports: After the formal ceremonies, the Heads of State, representatives of foreign governments, members of the Royal Family and the officials offered scarves and presents to the young King.

Later the ruler was ceremoniously carried in a palanquin to the Royal Cottage down below the palace on the bank of Thimphu Chhu River.

In the evening, the King hosted a buffet dinner to the Heads of States, diplomats and other dignitaries.

The Bhutanese Posts and Telegraphs Department brought out special coronation stamps, including scented stamps with floral motifs on the occasion. Stamps happen to be the kingdom's largest foreign exchange earner and Bhutan is perhaps the first in the world of philately to introduce the three dimensional stamps.

Also perhaps for the first time, Bhutanese currency notes up to ten Ngultrums (equivalent of ten Indian Rupees) were put into circulation by the Bank of Bhutan.

Mrs. Gandhi's Message

The Prime Minister, Mrs. Indira Gandhi, in a message to King Jigme Singye Wangchuck today, wished him a long and successful reign and said she took satisfaction from close understanding and co-operation between the two countries and looked forward to further expansion of friendly relations.

China congratulated the King on his coronation, Peking's official news agency reported. This was done in a message signed by the acting President Tung Pi-wu and Premier Chou Enlai yesterday. The message wished Bhutan new successes in safeguarding national independence and in ensuring its people's well-being and prosperity.

Opposite page: The sacred Guru Thongdrel unfurled on June 2, 1974 for the coronation of His Majesty the fourth Druk Gyalpo.

Asahi Shimbun   February 28, 1989

Mingling with Dignitaries Meeting with Japanese People

King of Bhutan's Active 'Royal Diplomacy' During Week in Tokyo

Reported by Akira Sasaki

Among the official delegations from 164 countries attending Emperor Hirohito's funeral was the Royal mission from the small Himalayan Kingdom of Bhutan, led by King Jigme Singye Wangchuck. It was reported that, upon hearing of the passing of the Japanese Emperor last month, King Wangchuck promptly ordered state mourning and personally hosted a special Buddhist service for the Emperor at the temple inside his palace.

While in Tokyo, the King, always in kimono-like traditional dress, was seen actively engaging in formal and informal meetings with international and Japanese dignitaries. These are some of the events during the four-day stay in Tokyo of the world's youngest monarch, who was on his first visit to Japan.

The delegation, aboard a British-made 80-passenger aircraft, Royal Bhutan Airline's only jetliner, arrived in Tokyo's Haneda Airport in the early evening of February 22, after an overnight stay in Hong Kong. The 11-member delegation included Mr. Keiji

Nishioka, an agriculture expert sent to Bhutan from Japan International Cooperation Agency who has been working in Bhutan for over 20 years now.

King Wangchuck during his stay had meetings extensively with the members of Japan's Imperial Family, including the Emperor and Empress, and His Imperial Highness the Crown Prince who went to visit Bhutan in 1987, along with leaders of the Japanese government.

Despite the busy schedule, the King managed to sit down with His Royal Highness Crown Prince Maha Vajiralongkorn of Thailand, the official delegation from Korea, as well as other international dignitaries.

"While some visiting Asian VIPs rather quickly initiated discussing such details as the amount of Japan's economic assistance, etc., I was very much impressed by His Majesty the King of Bhutan, who had a clear idea of nation building best suited to his country, putting the importance on his people's self

reliance," said Ambassador Kensuke Yanagiya, President of JICA.

Meanwhile, members of the Japan-Bhutan Friendship Association provided the delegation with flowers and fruits and presented the King 1,000 sets of picture postcards that were made of the photographs taken by its members in Bhutan. The King granted an extraordinary audience to the association's president, Mr. Kinya Niizeki, and other board members.

On the eve of returning to Bhutan, the King talked to the press for the first time, sitting with this reporter. The Bhutanese monarch expressed his respect to the late Emperor, whose greatness was felt throughout the funeral. The King also stressed his respect of and interest in Japan's achievements in economic development, referring to possibilities in joint research of natural resources in the Kingdom and possible joint ventures to make efficient use of mineral and other resources in the near future.

Opposite page: His Majesty with Japan's Crown Prince Naruhito during the prince's visit to Bhutan in 1987.

Time Magazine   December 21, 1998 Vol. 152 No. 24

A King's Life: Meditation and Hoops

By Tim McGirk, Thimphu

As a youngster, Jigme Singye Wangchuck stopped playing goalie in soccer when he realised that none of the players dared to knock one past the future King of Bhutan. So he switched to a more egalitarian sport: basketball, where the game's fast pace and sharp elbows tend to blur any distinction between royalty and commoners. His jumpshots on the public courts of Thimphu ended abruptly in 1972 when his father died, and Jigme, then 17, became the world's youngest monarch. Yet after about a quarter-century as ruler of the Thunder Dragon people, he is still a team player. This summer he agreed to relinquish some of his sovereign powers.

"We're hemmed in between two of the most populous and powerful nations on earth – India and China – and it's important that people realise the future survival of Bhutan doesn't depend on any single individual," the King told TIME. The elected National Assembly now has the right to demand his abdication in a confidence vote, if that's what the Bhutanese people want. It's unlikely to occur. To use a metaphor the King would appreciate, it would be like asking Chicago Bulls fans if they wanted Michael Jordan to hang up his sneakers.

While other kingdoms have vanished across the Himalayas – Tibet fell to China, Ladakh and Sikkim were engulfed by India – King Jigme has preserved Bhutan's independence and cultural heritage. His subjects now live longer, earn more and eat better than ever, and they receive free education and health care. Certain strictures, like obliging men to wear traditional robes, are a small price to pay. The King still plays hoops with his palace guards: at 1.8 m, he's a playmaker and three-point shooter. He is also accessible: any Bhutanese citizen can receive an audience.

King Jigme has four wives, all of whom are sisters. ("It wouldn't work if we weren't sisters," one Queen once explained. "There would be too much rivalry.") Every night, though, he retires to a simple, two-storey log cabin where he works until late. "His Majesty has no desire for material wealth," says a cabinet minister. "He would have made an excellent lama."

When the King first began touring Bhutan, people were too awestruck to confront him about their needs. "He told his ministers to goad the villagers into speaking out," says a civil servant. These days, he is besieged with demands. The King is oddly reticent, however, when asked what makes him content. "Happiness isn't that important to me," he says. "It's enough that I can achieve my responsibilities to strengthen Bhutan and give it a bright future." For the moment, satisfaction found in the swish of a three-pointer will have to suffice for the ruler of the Thunder Dragon people.

Opposite page: His Majesty the fourth Druk Gyalpo has preserved Bhutan's independence and cultural heritage.

Time Magazine   December 21, 1998 Vol. 152 No. 24

Asiaweek   September 27, 1985

Thunder Dragon King:
King Jigme Singye Wangchuck

The King of Bhutan agreed to an interview with Asiaweek in September

By Ravi Vellore, Thimphu

Q: What is your outlook for Bhutan in the 21st Century?

King Jigme: Being a least developed country and land-locked, with a small population, does put a somewhat different picture to our aspirations and objectives. But the most important thing is to remain a sovereign, independent country and to continue to enjoy peace and harmony. Time is essential to us.

In the last 24 years, our stress has been on rapid development. We find now that one aspect we have neglected is the social/cultural factor. Per capita income is not the only thing. We'll have the highest per capita income in South Asia by the end of our sixth plan – ending in 1991. Development is important, but preserving our own culture is equally important. Our religion, our culture, and our values have given us centuries of peace and stability. These aspects have not always been fully taken into consideration. There has been a blind and haphazard approach to development. The social side is now given top priority, but we certainly do not want to be seen as a showpiece of the 17th and 18th centuries.

Q: How would you compare yourself with His Late Majesty? Where have you gone forward from your father's thinking?

I don't see any essential breakage from my father's line of thinking. With the changing times some policies necessarily have to change. My father began the development process. In my time, there has been consolidation of the government, with emphasis on the creation of a small and efficient administration. What is important is to face challenges that will arise, and it is my job to produce and display the necessary qualities of leadership to my people. This year has been earmarked as the year for consolidation of government.

Q: You seem to be personally isolated. Why is it that you rarely travel outside Bhutan?

I do not have the urge to travel outside Bhutan. I think the best place to have a holiday is Bhutan itself. We haven't really got this legacy of protocol, so we can afford to mix with people at all levels, be relaxed. There is no threat to personal security. We are slowly beginning to take precautions though.

And, no, I don't feel isolated. Bhutan and Thimphu are such small places; everyone is within reach. And I can always call in some officials. We have excellent relations with the King of Nepal. I shall be going there later this year.

Q: Do you regret not having had the benefit of a fuller education?

It is too late for regret. It is a fait accompli. Obviously, if my father didn't have his heart problems, I'd have liked that better. But you can't change the past. I knew nothing when I became king; although a year before his death my father did ask me in for cabinet meetings. I was completely new. The learning process lasted about four to five years. Even now I'm learning though.

Q: What about marriage? People in town say the Je Khenpo – head lama – has advised you that the time is not propitious yet. They are looking forward to a week's marriage festivities.

Yes. I'm under heavy pressure from various quarters to choose a queen. I guess I'll have to do something about that soon. No, the Je Khenpo has not advised anything like that. In any case, we do not consult the lama on such things. As for festivities, a landlocked LDC – least developed country – cannot waste money on functions that do not help people.

Q: Do you contemplate any diffusion of your absolute power, a turn towards democracy?

We are searching very, very hard for our own system. We are not led by models. We have studied the Westminster system and have seen its drawbacks. The form of government we have now is young and without preconceived notions. We realise that change is necessary. The king's contribution should be what is most useful for the people of Bhutan.

If you care to observe, there has been a very interesting evolution of monarchy in Bhutan. The National Assembly was created in 1954, but the representatives were too worried, too introverted. They wouldn't speak out. Then we said we'd have 105 people's representatives, plus 12 from the clergy and 33 from the government. In the last 13 years, the National Assembly has been the most important policy-making body. All legislation, even cabinet decisions can be reversed or changed.

In the spring of 1984 we set up the Royal Advisory Council, which includes six members from the people, two from the government and two from the clergy, to act as watchdogs. The RAC has the power to not only advise the king, but also report to the National Assembly if they find the king going against the national interest. The king would then have to defend himself before the National Assembly; I said, there is no danger in this. However, none of the devolution of powers has been done deliberately. We are still searching very hard for 'our own' system.

Q: What has stopped you from establishing diplomatic relations with China?

Diplomatic relations alone are not of great importance to our sovereignty. One or a hundred missions makes no difference. China is a big country and we seek good relations with her. But right now our priority is to demarcate our northern border. We feel confident that it is a matter of time before our relations grow still better and this problem is finally settled.

Yes, I agree with you; there are many people, especially in northern Bhutan, who would like to have ties re-established with China. So far, only two dzongkhas in the area have raised the issue, and for trade reasons only. You see, we grow everything that Tibet does not grow.

Q: Your stand on Cambodia – in support of the Democratic Coalition – brings you close to ASEAN. Why do you not seek closer ties with them?

Yes, our stand on Cambodia is a small step forward. We are against any country invading any country by use of force. We felt that Vietnam invaded Cambodia and so we have to condemn the act.

Asiaweek   September 27, 1985

Self-determination should be left to the people of Cambodia. It was a matter of principle.

We would like to develop ties with the ASEAN nations, because, after all, we are all Asian. Also, in today's world, trade is the key. Markets are very, very important to us. This goes for both South Asia and Southeast Asia, as well as West Asia. Although rather new, we have excellent ties with the ASEAN and we are progressing slowly on this.

Q: Your country recently signed the nuclear non-proliferation treaty. Why did you decide to back it?

We feel strongly for such a treaty, because it has aspects [in it] we felt were good for humankind. In such aspects, we wish to follow an active foreign policy.

Q: Have you ever considered declaring Bhutan a zone of peace? How do you react to Nepal's proposal to declare itself a zone of peace?

We in Bhutan have never thought about this for ourselves. Our prime consideration is to continue to remain a sovereign country. What's more important [than such proposals] is the question of being efficient, capable to meet situations, to be nationalistic. Hence the emphasis we place on education.

I'm going to Nepal later this year. They have never approached us with a peace zone proposal. If they do, well, we'll have to hold a cabinet meeting. My own thinking? Well, my own thinking would be to abide by the decision of my cabinet (laughing).

Q: What did you feel when Sikkim acceded – some say it was annexed – to India in 1975? Did you fear that a similar thing might happen here?

We had close ties with the Chogyal of Sikkim. We are slightly related, too. At the time we felt bad for the Chogyal. But there is an essential difference in the status of Sikkim and Bhutan. We isolated ourselves because of the British presence in India. Sikkim did not. Naturally, after the British left, their status differed from ours – they became a protectorate. The Indian Resident in Gangtok was concurrently accredited as only a 'political officer' for Bhutan, and he would visit us once in a long while. So you see the difference. That's why we are not alarmed whether Sikkim acceded or was annexed by India. If the people of Sikkim want to become a part of India, it's up to them. It's strictly their business.

Time   April 30, 2006

Jigme Singye Wangchuck

Bhutan's King, now 50, suggests that nations be measured by 'Gross National Happiness'; the rich are not always happy

By Pico Iyer

King Jigme Singye Wangchuck, great grandson of Bhutan's first hereditary monarch and once the world's youngest King (when he came to power in 1972), rules his people more in the spirit of Buddha than of more worldly princes. To this day there is not a traffic light in the Himalayan Kingdom, by law everyone must wear traditional 14th century clothing and the number of tourists allowed into the country over the past 10 years is lower than the number of fans who pile into a college football game.

Television and the Internet have, it is true, arrived with the 21st Century, and a few superluxe hotels are now coming up around Bhutan, but what hits you when you touch down in its only airport is the silence.

Almost 30 years ago, long before 'positive psychology' became a boom in the West, King Jigme, now 50, suggested that nations be measured by 'Gross National Happiness'; the rich are not always happy, after all, while the happy generally consider themselves rich. Four months ago, he launched an even more radical idea: self-deposition.

To urge his people toward independence, he announced that he would step down two years from now (his son would officially take over) and that his country would hold its first national democratic elections.

King Jigme—who gave up absolute power in 1998 and last year sent every household in the land a new draft constitution that allowed for his impeachment—is setting a quietly revolutionary precedent. If most politicians are inherently suspect because they seem so eager to grab power and so reluctant to surrender it, what does one make of a leader who voluntarily gives up his position, as if placing his people's needs before his own?

Opposite page: The historic Trongsa Dzong.

The New York Times   March 23, 1991

Thimphu Journal: Bhutan's King Doth Protest. Now Is It Too Much?

By Barbara Crossette
Special to *The New York Times* from Thimphu, Bhutan

"The flaw in monarchy," the King of Bhutan said, "is that you reach that very high and important position not due to merit, but due to birth. Too much depends on one individual."

His Majesty Jigme Singye Wangchuck, the Druk Gyalpo, or Precious Ruler of the Dragon People, and the last of the Himalayan Buddhist kings, has been thinking a lot about monarchy and its role in a world swept by democracy movements. On the shoulders of this 35-year-old basketball-playing ruler rests the responsibility of modernising Bhutan, an exotic land sealed off from the rest of the world for most of its existence. Dressed in a silk kimono called a kho, a gold sword at his side, the King said in a recent interview that he spends 80 percent of his time reading prosaic files.

Environmental causes, industrial projects, plans for a new television network or a new self-defense militia all land on his desk. The rest of the time is spent traveling this rugged country nestled between China and India, sitting down for meals with villagers and listening to their jokes and their concerns.

The People, Not the King

"I don't think Bhutan's political future, and the well-being of our people, our security and our sovereignty, can be determined by one individual," the King said. "I always stress in all my speeches and talks to school children that the future of Bhutan does not lie in the hands of the King. The future of Bhutan lies in the hands of the Bhutanese people."

The King, a serious man who is fourth in a dynasty installed in 1907 but heir to a 1,300-year-old Bhutanese tradition, insists that his family never had any intention of retaining absolute power in this landlocked country,

and that the country's education policies alone prove this.

"If the Government and the previous kings of Bhutan wanted to keep Bhutan on a feudal basis, we would have never given priority to mass education, and definitely not in English," he said, sitting in a corner of a royal audience hall furnished in woven silk and snow-leopard pelts, which he hastened to explain were put there long before his reign. Across the room, a gilded throne, empty, glowed in the sun.

The challenge is making the transition from near-medieval monarchy to a durable new form of government without disrupting tradition or creating instability.

A Place Unto Itself

The experiences of European constitutional monarchies have little relevance to this land of 600,000 people whose lives revolve around alpine meadows and ancient monasteries called dzongs, enveloped in incense and the hum of monks chanting scripture and prayers.

Far to the northeast, the Emperor of Japan, whose coronation the Bhutanese King attended, also lives in a different world. In Thailand, however, he finds a kindred soul, King Bhumibol Adulyadej, who devotes himself to development projects and the support of Thai culture.

"I have never had the honour and privilege of meeting the King of Thailand," the King of Bhutan said, "but I have always wanted to pay my respects to him. What work he has done is something very admirable in a very, very difficult situation politically."

Bhutan's ruler, heir of a Tibetan Tantric Buddhist tradition unique to the Himalayas, has put religion on his agenda for reform. Under his reign, which began in

1972, when he was only 19, thousands of monks have acquired life insurance and pension plans. Relations between King and clergy are harmonious, he said.

Monks Must Adapt

"But even within Buddhism, certain changes have to take place," the King went on. "Monks can no longer, like in the past, live in the four corners of the dzongs, but will have to go out and do social work. We would like them to be doctors, be health workers, help the farmers, help the poor people. I think that in this day and age, the Buddhist institutions in Bhutan will have to reach out to the people."

The King went to schools in India and Britain before returning to Bhutan in 1971 to study under tutors and help his father, King Jigme Dorji Wangchuck, who was ill. He said he knew nothing about kingship when he inherited the throne the following year.

"To be very frank, when my father died in 1972, there was very, very little that I knew about the governing of the country," he said. "People thought that, well, he must have lot of experience because he was there with his father all the time. But in reality I didn't know what Bhutan's foreign policy was, I didn't know what Bhutan's national objectives were, I didn't know what Bhutan's problems were, I didn't know what the Bhutan Government's priorities were."

Life will be different for Crown Prince Jigme Khesar Namgyel Wangchuck, one of eight children of the King's four wives, who are sisters.

"As for my son — he just became 11 on the 21st of February – I am trying to give him a normal life and a normal education," the King said. "I'm going to make him study in schools in Bhutan, and without any special privileges. He should not be separated from the problems or the way of life of the Bhutanese people."

Opposite page: His Majesty the fourth Druk Gyalpo on the golden throne.

Bhutan is Ready for Democracy

In his first interview in six years, King Jigme Singye Wangchuck of Bhutan spoke to Sanjoy Hazarika about his vision for his tiny land and its people, the need for multi-party democracy, his roll-back of near-absolute powers for himself and the monarchy and the efforts to negotiate the departure of militants from the North-east, which failed, and the military action which followed. The King's initiative to slash his own authority is little short of revolutionary. He retains control of the Royal Bhutan Army, which saw military action for the first time in December and which is bound to have a major role in Bhutan, given heightened threat perceptions. Over the past years, a Council of Ministers has evolved with new, young faces all of whom are elected by the National Assembly.

On democratic changes in Bhutan and the draft Constitution

The reason that the Constitution is being drafted is because Bhutan and its people are ready to have a democratic political system. And it will be based on parliamentary democracy. After the Constitution is drafted, I am going to go to all 20 districts to consult local leaders and villagers and explain to them the Constitution – what it means – since party politics is something that is alien to our people. Clause by clause, article by article, it will be discussed with scholars and villagers, with the business and finance community and with all the people. For us in Bhutan, the most important thing is to have good governance. I want a democratic political system that will provide good governance. Can we succeed in this or not is difficult to say, because it is a new experience for all of us. It depends on the Bhutanese people and how politically mature they will be and the responsibilities they will take. This is a process of referendum, it will take time, there will be opposition, some because people do not understand, also some because they see a new system. We know that party political systems which have come up in developing countries have often not done well.

On the role of the King

The King will be a constitutional head. This is something that we want to do. There is no pressure on me at all, certainly not from within the country. But right from the 1970s, I realised that Bhutan cannot have a different political system than what prevails in the South Asian Association for Regional Cooperation. The only factor here is a democratic political system that works, that provides stability and good governance. To say that this process is 'too early' is not an argument; it is an excuse for not doing it. I do not believe in these excuses.

On contacts with the NE militants

The problem started in 1990/1991 with Operation Rhino and Bajrang (of the Indian Army against the militants). We did not know anything about the Ulfa; NDFB-KLO did not even exist at the time. They did not come deep inside but stayed on the Assam-Bhutan border. From 1991-94, many Indian Army operations were launched to remove these people after I gave permission. The result was that instead of leaving, they started going deep within Bhutan and that created the problem for us. We believed that we could resolve this peacefully because of good relations with Assam, and we believed that they could not have an independent Assam and Bodoland. For six years, we tried to have a dialogue with them and did not succeed. In Bhutan, the responsibility of safeguarding the security and integrity of the kingdom is the responsibility of the King. I told the National Assembly that (I would do) whatever it takes to fulfill this responsibility and, in all sincerity, I tried my best to resolve the problem peacefully by talking to them.

I met the leadership in the camps. I went to practically all their camps. It was not easy for them to come for a dialogue, they said. KLO never came here for a dialogue. I went without security and without being announced, without a big entourage, to these heavily fortified camps where they had been living for years. I talked to NDFB, Ulfa, KLO and tried to reason with them and explain to them, but they were not responsive. They wanted the independence of Assam and Bodoland. I said, "How can you have two independent states, including Bodoland inside Assam?" I told them this was impractical since they were surrounded by Indian states. They gave the example of East Timor. I was not successful in convincing them.

On criticism that Bhutan should have taken action earlier

What many people simply overlooked was that these people – call them militants, terrorists or anti-nationals – were Indian nationals. To launch an operation against Indian nationals was difficult. We have such good relations with Assam going back a thousand years. We were very concerned that this would have strong repercussions on Assam and our relations with Assam. From what we hear, there is a lot of relief and appreciation that people do not have to pay taxes to the militants, which were being collected earlier. Very large amounts were collected from Assam and from Assamese working in Bhutan. What many people forget is that there are only three road links between Bhutan and the rest of the world: all of them go through India. We are totally dependent on these routes, two of which go through Assam including the Bodo areas. All our trade, our oranges, ginger and cardamom is transported through these routes. We tried to stop Bhutanese from trading with the militants; it affected all our border towns and markets. Not one shop was left open, and it caused a lot of economic hardship. We supplied goods to people from the Food Corporation of Bhutan godowns, but the media reported militants starving and in poor conditions. This was not true. They had plenty of money.

On relations with India

A good thing about being around for 32 years is that whatever government comes to power in Delhi, you will see many familiar faces! For us it is important that India has a stable government.

The author is a consulting editor with *The Statesman*.

Opposite page: Crowds pack the Changlimithang stadium for National Day celebrations.

The Statesman

December 21, 2006

Bhutan Abdication
An Extraordinary Step Without Pomp or Self-Congratulation

By Salman Haidar
India's former Foreign Secretary

The most arresting development in present day South Asia is King Jigme Singye Wangchuck of Bhutan's abdication from the throne in favour of his son. Suddenly, the region's longest serving ruler, a popular and respected statesman, has quit the scene.

It has been an orderly transition, meticulously orchestrated, long anticipated but yet a shock and a surprise, for the King had been there for so long that the idea of someone else now taking over is not easily absorbed. Moreover, though the decision had been made known some time ago, the actual abdication took place rather earlier than anticipated. Typical of the former King, this extraordinary step was taken without pomp or self-congratulation – just a swift action when nobody was looking for it, leaving behind a slightly stunned populace.

Nothing compelled the King to give up his throne. He had reigned for thirty-four years, was fit and active, his people's cynosure. Bhutan developed steadily under his leadership, transforming itself from a simple, remote society shrinking from the world into a more complex, self-confident realm capable of handling the external challenges it must face.

A Buddhist Kingdom

While doing so, it has maintained its distinctiveness as a Buddhist Kingdom — the last of its type anywhere — and strengthened its national identity. It has opened up peacefully, at its own pace and in its own manner, choosing a form of development that has made it a byword for environmental sensitivity.

His abdication was no impulsive act. For a quarter of a century or more, the King had been shedding the absolute authority of his high position, devolving more and more power to the state structures set up for the purpose, pushing his officials to take more responsibility.

He progressively gave up the prerogative of making appointments, entrusting the task to a state commission. District officials were invested with an authority they had never enjoyed in earlier years, initially with mixed results, as poorly trained and sometimes corrupt officials took advantage of the situation.

But things settled down. The National Assembly was strengthened and encouraged to keep an eye on the administration. The ministers and their supporting officials became more prominent and were organised in a cabinet under a rotating Prime Minister. The law was codified and a proper Supreme Court established.

And when all these and other basic attributes of a modern state were put in place, a constitution was drafted under which the monarchy itself would become a constitutional structure. This sweeping transition has been widely explained to the people of Bhutan, whose acceptance of the projected arrangements is crucial to their success.

The monarch, and his late father before him, realised early that Bhutan's security and future prosperity lay in going with the democratic tide rather than resisting it. Few ruling monarchs worldwide showed comparable acumen. Yet Bhutan's people were not yet politically aware and were attached to the monarchy with which they were familiar, so had to be led and persuaded to accept something different. It has taken many years, but now, despite some uneasiness at moving out of the shadow of the only ruler most of them have ever known, everything suggests that the people of Bhutan are ready for the next phase in the transformation of their country.

Bhutan is held up as a model among India's neighbours, a country with which India has an exemplary relationship. India has done much to develop and sustain this relationship. Jawaharlal Nehru himself went to Bhutan, at a time when the journey required days of travel on horseback. In Bhutan, he underwrote the country's entire development plan and helped launch its modernisation. Following Nehru's lead, India has always tried to be generous and supportive, and has acquiesced in the gradual emergence of Bhutan from under its shadow.

Ties with India

The great disproportion in size and capacity between the two countries has not prevented the growth of close and harmonious relations. They have been able to collaborate on large hydro-electric projects that have transformed the relationship and given vast benefits to each, though initially some Bhutanese officials felt the projects were too big and would subordinate Bhutan's interest to that of India.

Another critical development was the successful strike at armed camps set up in Bhutan by insurgent Indian groups. Such major actions were the hallmark of the King's dealings with India, acting boldly and independently when the time was ripe, working with his large neighbour where common interests prevailed.

Bhutan's new monarch is now on the throne, H.M. King Jigme Khesar Namgyel Wangchuck. He is very familiar with India, with a wide range of friends in this country and the benefit of a year at the National Defence College in New Delhi. He will preside over the transition to popular rule in 2008 under the new constitution.

At that time, a more clamorous Assembly may well emerge, more inclined to take a critical look at government policy, including relations with India. New Delhi can view the prospect with equanimity, for the India-Bhutan relationship has been well launched and remains in good hands.

Opposite page: The fourth Druk Gyalpo leads Bhutan towards democracy.

Photo: courtesy Lyonpo Sangay Ngedup • following pages courtesy Indian Embassy, Thimphu

Gross National Happiness is far more important than Gross National Product.

His Majesty Jigme Singye Wangchuck

Chapter Five

The World Remembers

Enlightened Monarchy

Never in the history of human endeavour, relating to the small nation state, has so much been done by just one person for the enduring benefit of so many people! Further, those people who have benefited are not just Bhutanese, but people beyond the Kingdom of Bhutan, indeed right around the world.

I refer, of course, to the fourth King of Bhutan, the King Father of Bhutan, and I apologise to Sir Winston Churchill for borrowing his famous World War Two phrase, but it fits the bill relating to this extraordinary man who voluntarily abdicated in favour of his son, H.R.H. the Crown Prince, late last year.

On one occasion, as I entered the royal reception room in Thimphu to meet His Majesty, I was struck by the awe of his presence: a quiet dignity and determination, a wisdom on many matters of challenge to Bhutan and the world. Further, the surrounds were very modest, in keeping with the then King's focus and uncluttered ways.

His contributions are very many, including the concept of Gross National Happiness, and it is to his everlasting credit that this has been successfully webbed into the fabric of the Kingdom of Bhutan, enhancing national well-being in the process. Indeed it is now being closely studied worldwide. Variations of GNH are being adopted in places a long way from Bhutan, including Australia and Canada.

I salute His Majesty, the King Father, as a person who it has been a privilege to meet, as a person who fronted up bravely when required to deal with the Assam rebels in the southern forests of Bhutan and as a person who has brought much goodness to a troubled world.

As Bhutan completes 100 years with a designated enlightened monarchy, 1,000 years and more as an enlightened cultural wonderland in the southern Himalayan medicine valleys, it shines as a glistening pebble between two giant stones. That this is so, much is owed to the King Father, the fourth King, and also on a smaller scale to the fifth King. Long may the goodness of Bhutan reign!

The Hon. Tim Fischer AC
Former Deputy Prime Minister of Australia
2007

Opposite page: His Majesty the fourth Druk Gyalpo inspects a guard of honour at the Rashtrapati Bhavan in Delhi.

A Universally Loved Monarch

Our friendship with Bhutan began in 1948 when my wife was at school in London with the future Queen Mother, Ashi Keysang. We made our first journey there in 1967, followed by several visits since.

We first met His Majesty the fourth Druk Gyalpo when he was at school in England, and then watched the building of a school in Paro, which he attended on his return from England. Due to the very early death of his kind and far-sighted father, His Majesty came to the throne as a very young man. From the very beginning of his reign His Majesty showed tolerance and wisdom.

During the thirty-four years of his reign, through his policy of gentleness and resolve, he brought the country from being an isolated mountain kingdom into the 21st Century. Bhutan is now a member of the United Nations. The country now enjoys modern facilities; there is now a legal system, medical and educational institutions. All these developments were achieved without in any way compromising Bhutan's traditions and very exceptional characteristics.

With the co-operation of such countries as Switzerland and Denmark, His Majesty has been able to build a solid infrastructure in his kingdom. He has also maintained contact with the wider world. It cannot have been easy to represent an independent Bhutan, being surrounded by such large neighbours.

Throughout his reign, His Majesty Jigme Singye Wangchuck has managed, in an increasingly turbulent world, to remain a universally loved monarch whose unselfish aim to distribute 'Gross National Happiness' is an example to all those in power today. It is no small testament to his acumen that Bhutan should be preparing for its first ever general elections in 2008.

John Goelet
A Friend of Bhutan
2007

Sensitive Mind and Modern Outlook

In the contemporary world of changing political systems, it is not often that one comes across a personality like that of His Majesty Jigme Singye Wangchuck, the King of Bhutan, whose sensitive mind and modern outlook sustain the unity of the state and obtain the loyalty of the people.

I feel that the people of Bhutan are lucky to have His Majesty Jigme Singye Wangchuck at the helm at a time of rapid change of nations and societies due to continuing strides of science, technology and multimedia. Bhutan is no longer Shangri-La. It is a nation modernising itself under the direct leadership of a man of vision who is not tempted by the glitter of borrowed modernism, but has the wisdom to find a judicious balance between the traditional and the modern. Under His Majesty's guidance, Bhutan has arrived from the edge of time to the mainstream of global change. While its visions of the future are riveted on the great heights of the mighty Himalayas, in whose bosom it nestles, its feet are firmly on the earth that has sustained the Kingdom since it was created as a unified political entity in the 17th Century. There may be no country like Bhutan that so well combines change with stability, the new with the ancient. The credit goes to the King as well as the people of Bhutan. The people are gentle, honest and hard-working. Their King laces power with compassion and humility.

My personal acquaintance with the Kingdom of Bhutan goes back to the coronation of His Majesty. The golden occasion was celebrated with Bhutan's typical mingle of austerity and appropriate extravaganza; the solemnity of the occasion made almost more poetic by the youth of the new King and the dignity with which he ascended the throne. The year was 1974 and the new monarch was just 19 years of age. Since then I have had the pleasure of visiting Thimphu and other places several times and the honour of an abiding personal friendship with the King. I chose Thimphu as the first foreign capital to visit when I became Prime Minister of India in March, 1997.

Impressions and Tributes

During his reign, Bhutan has grown from almost a pastoral economy to a steadily modernising one, while its monarch has grown from a visionary youth to a mature person who is still young and, happily, has many, many years to pilot his Kingdom through the inevitable turmoil of growth and modernisation. His matured youth has acquired some of the wisdom that is native to the Himalayas. He has drawn from the eternal storehouse of wisdom of the ever-enduring teachings of Gautama Buddha. Mixing caution with dynamism, at times with radicalism, he has brought his Kingdom to a stage when it has a surplus budget; finds most of its development funds from its own resources; has built and is still engaged in building institutions of the state as the habitat of a people on the move from one milestone of growth and development to another; and is steadily widening its horizons in education, health and freedom from want, as well as in political, economic and social development.

I have watched with admiration how the King of Bhutan has navigated the shoals of development. Bhutan is the most stable country in South Asia and in much of the wider world. He has not allowed Bhutan's lavish wealth of forests to be ravished in the name of development. He has not allowed the fresh air and pure water of the rivers and rivulets flowing down from the Himalayas to be spoiled in the name of tourism. The big power plant at Chukha and the bigger one that is being built at Tala, both with India's co-operation, provide enough electricity for Bhutan's confident strides forward in the new millennium.

King Jigme Singye Wangchuck has crafted a process of democratisation on Bhutan's own cultural and civilisational tracks. From the village to the district to the national level, Bhutan is governed by elected representatives of its own people. It is they who determine the priorities of development. Never colonised by the British, Bhutan has not tried to graft a foreign political model on its rocky and, at the same time, green pastures. Last year, the King delegated all executive power to the cabinet, and much against its will, persuaded the National Assembly to put before the people, for a whole year's debate, a royal Kasho which makes it obligatory for the Parliament to express, in total freedom, its confidence in the monarch himself. If the vote of confidence does not pass, the monarch will step down in favour of the Crown Prince. Bhutan, then, is building its own democracy in accordance with its own design, with its own characteristics.

Bhutan is India's closest neighbour, friend and ally. Its foreign policy is anchored on non-alignment. It has been playing an important role in SAARC since the creation of the regional body. Bhutan has long borders with Asia's two largest countries, India and China. Both borders have remained peaceful and tranquil.

I began by saying that the people of Bhutan are fortunate in having as their monarch a man who has attributes of Plato's philosopher-king. Let me end by saying that India is fortunate in having Bhutan and its young, dynamic, wise and progressive King as its closest neighbour and friend. I wish His Majesty Jigme Singye Wangchuck a very long and active life engaged in one of the most fruitful models of political and social engineering of our time.

HE Mr. I.K. Gujral, MP
Former Prime Minister of India
1999

Reprinted from *25 Years a King*, The National Steering Committee for the Royal Silver Jubilee Celebrations, 1999.

Tribute to His Majesty, the Fourth Druk Gyalpo

Our friendship with the people of Bhutan has brought my family great joy, and we are deeply appreciative to the Royal Family for a lifetime of memories. Now shared by the fourth generation, the relationship began when Her Majesty Ashi Kesang and I were classmates in England. We have seen Bhutan emerge into a state respected worldwide for its cultural preservation and environmental leadership.

As a young child, His Majesty travelled with his family to visit my parents and me at our home in Switzerland, naming it the 'Swiss Dzong'. A strong friendship grew between my father, Fritz von Schulthess, and His Majesty's father. We spoke of the similarities between our countries and of His Late Majesty's dreams for modernising Bhutan. My family continues to regularly visit Bhutan and to welcome Bhutanese into our homes in New York and Boston.

We have watched Bhutan flourish under the enlightened leadership of His Majesty Jigme Singye Wangchuck and are full of admiration for his astute balance of tradition and development. Following the path of his visionary concept of Gross National Happiness, in just a few decades, his introduction of education, health care, hydro power and many other initiatives has dramatically improved the quality of life of Bhutan's citizens. The extended Hoch family congratulates His Majesty on his successful reign, and we send best wishes for an auspicious beginning to the reign of His Majesty the fifth King and the upcoming elections in 2008.

Lisina von Schulthess Hoch and family
A Friend of Bhutan
2007

Opposite page: His Majesty, H.R.H. Ashi Dechen Wangmo Wangchuck and Indian president Fakhruddin Ali Ahmed at a state banquet in Delhi in December 1974.

A Tribute to His Majesty Jigme Singye Wangchuck

Much will be written about His Majesty Jigme Singye Wangchuck's awesome accomplishments as a leader and statesman who has steered his country from a relatively backward and isolated kingdom to an economically secure and vibrant modern nation, and then voluntarily devolved his virtually absolute powers to democratic institutions of governance. Much will also be written of his singular contribution in building the exemplary relations between his country and India.

During my tenure as Ambassador to Bhutan in the late nineties, the King steered to successful conclusion the three major agreements regarding the Tala and Kurichu hydroelectric projects and the Dungsum cement project, as well as other significant projects concerning India's economic assistance to Bhutan. He also masterminded and then personally conducted the decisive and brilliant military operations against Indian militants from Assam and West Bengal, who had illegally established camps in Bhutan and posed a grave security risk to both countries. As he has often told me, there is a geopolitical logic to this relationship that makes it unalterable. The King has interacted with almost every Prime Minister of India, all of whom have held him in the highest esteem as a true and loyal friend, and a leader of rare wisdom and compassion.

Yet when all is said about His Majesty's remarkable achievements, it is his human qualities and far-sighted vision that strike me as truly exceptional and rare. His ability to empathise with his people, to relate to their problems, is a trait that only truly great leaders have. He has always given priority to the human aspects of his responsibilities, for instance in not making economic growth an end in itself but rather the means for securing the happiness of his people. Equally admirable is the manner in which he has protected the pristine environment and the spectacular flora and fauna of Bhutan, through policies that were far ahead of their times. There are valuable lessons for all of us in Bhutan's neighbourhood in the environmental protection policies framed by His Majesty and in his holistic vision for the development and progress of his country. His wholehearted and unswerving commitment to the well-being of his country and his people have given His Majesty a moral authority, which has enabled him to carry out his visionary policies even in the face of difficult and sometimes unpopular decisions.

I have had the honour of knowing His Majesty since the mid-seventies, soon after he ascended the throne. I have always been struck by his rejection of the trappings of office, the pomp and pageantry usually associated with monarchy. His lifestyle is frugal, living as he does in a modest log cabin, tucked away in a forest, uncluttered by material possessions. His Majesty's incisive and eclectic mind, his keen sense of observation and his mastery of facts and figures enable him to instantly get to the essence of things, from policies to personalities. He has a sensitive and deeply reflective personality and a delightful sense of humour. His amazing memory, even for small details, makes those fortunate enough to interact with him feel very special.

At a personal level, I shall never forget His Majesty's many kindnesses and thoughtful gestures, even long after I've retired. Nor those days, many years ago, when, as a young first secretary in the Indian mission, I played tennis with him on the courts of Changlimithang, nor the memorable fishing trips followed by convivial picnics and barbeques, when his remarkable ability to put his guests at ease would sometimes make me forget that my host was none other than the King of Bhutan.

Dalip Mehta
Former Ambassador of India to Bhutan
2007

The Great Development Architect

It raised high expectations when I received instructions from the Ministry of Foreign Affairs in Denmark to set up the first Danida office in Bhutan in the early 1990s. The Kingdom of Denmark had identified the Royal Kingdom of Bhutan as one of its priority development partners, and the challenge was to build up a programme that would cover the interest of both partners over a relatively short time span.

Soon it became clear that the partnership would develop smoothly and efficiently because of the development policies of Bhutan and the matching priorities of Denmark. His Majesty King Jigme Singye Wangchuck had, over the years, crafted a sound and prudent development strategy. His foresight had put equity, welfare (Gross National Happiness) and democratisation at the heart of the national development agenda, and the pace envisioned was harmonised with the capacity of the people to adapt to change.

To work and live in Bhutan under such circumstances became a privilege. The compact and efficient civil service was the perfect partner to a donor agency from a small country with virtues very similar to those prevailing in Bhutan. Drawing on inspiration from His Majesty, development plans and targets were set based on national interest, and partners were expected to adapt and support the national plans without heavy conditional ties. This was much in line with Danish development policies and to this day remains consistent with best practice in the international development arena.

Living and working as an expatriate in Bhutan became a happy and fruitful experience both in terms of work and social relations. The peaceful capital, the breathtaking nature and the friendliness of the people were all elements that blended into the daily life, while audiences with His Majesty became highly inspirational encounters that helped draft the future steps in the partnership between our nations.

What we see today is an impressive consequence of the policies set out several decades ago by King Jigme Dorji Wangchuck. Democracy is developing, people's welfare is advancing, and poverty and inequities are rapidly diminishing. Bhutan is defined as a developing country, but it is also very developed on its own terms.

Two memories take high seat from my time, and from many later visits, in Bhutan.

The Bhutanese people were interested in learning and adopting technological progress in the richer world and then using it to the best benefit of the country. But, unlike in Bhutan, spiritual values were not seen as a quality in the Western world. "You Westerners are rich in material things, but we Bhutanese are rich in spiritual values".

At a luncheon hosted by His Majesty, I asked him about the yeti in Bhutan. His Majesty answered that he had been trying to gain evidence of its presence in Bhutan. His Majesty had even sent out scouts with cameras to try to capture images of the yeti. Once, His Majesty told me, one of these scouts had come across a yeti, but he became so nervous that he was shaking all over when he took his picture, and it became so blurred that the creature could not be seen clearly. I believe that demonstrating the existence of the yeti is one of the only achievements in which His Majesty has not succeeded.

Bjorn Melgaard
Former Danida Co-ordinator in Bhutan
2007

A King of the People

During many of my visits to Bhutan as Chairman of the German NGO 'Pro Bhutan Association', I have enjoyed the great honour and privilege to be received by His Majesty King Jigme Singye Wangchuck.

His Majesty always graced our work in Bhutan and showed great interest in our humanitarian projects in rural health and education of disabled children, proving his care for and unrelenting commitment to the less privileged groups of Bhutanese people.

The audience His Majesty was so generous to grant my wife Angelika and me at the occasion of our marriage in Bhutan in 1999 turned out to be a wonderful experience.

It was His Majesty's weekly 'open day' for Bhutanese citizens of any walk of life. His Majesty received one person after another: an elderly peasant woman, bent by hard work in the fields, a desperate shopkeeper, a hopeful student, a young pregnant lady, a hesitant civil servant. Once in front of His Majesty, who received them standing, it seemed that, after performing their correct reverence and greeting ritual, they were petrified by their own audacity to approach their sovereign.

But His Majesty, slightly bowing his head to his Bhutanese subjects, radiated such natural friendliness, such benign and personal interest, that, seeing his caring smile, hearing his encouraging welcome, the shyness fell from the shoulders of the humble visitors like a heavy chain cloak. And they then felt free to submit to His Majesty their grievances or wishes. His Majesty listened attentively, asked one or two questions and gave his verdict or recommendation. Sometimes, His Majesty gave immediate orders to an ADC to follow up the case.

Witnessing the happy smile, the shining eyes, the exuberant gratefulness of the Bhutanese citizens taking reluctant leave of their beloved King, we were deeply touched: His Majesty thus gave proof that he was a real King of the people, and inspired life, also in this extraordinary way. His very own project of enhancing the 'Gross National Happiness' of his people in contrast to the 'golden calf' of 'Gross National Product' is now venerated everywhere in the world. We asked ourselves: where would there be another head of state with such a personal interest in his subjects and who shows such care for the well-being of his citizens?

Harald N. Nestroy
German Ambassador (retired)
Executive Chairman, Pro Bhutan Association
2007

Opposite page: Bhutanese citizens seek an audience with their king.

For All Time to Come

Just before sunrise on this tropical island that is my adopted home, the ocean breeze is translucent, gentle rain showers blessings, and birds sing their hearts out in anticipation of a beautiful day. It is my favourite time for a quiet reflection. And this morning was especially quiet and more reflective than ever.

The last Kasho (royal decree) of His Majesty the fourth Druk Gyalpo arrived on my laptop screen this morning. The Kasho's content did not surprise me. My sixth sense had told me – with an unusual clarity some time ago – that I must expect such an announcement, not in 2008, but on National Day 2006. This insight hit me like a thunderbolt, but I reflected on it a little and thought it quite logical, most reasonable and exceedingly wise.

In other words, I was fully prepared.

Yet, still, tracing every word of the Kasho over, and over and over again, brought the reality home. And tears to my eyes.

It is the singular hallmark of a great leader to know when to leave and to act on that knowledge when the time is right – and to do so for nothing other than a higher purpose, bigger than life.

There has been quite a few so-called 'great leaders' in the world's history. But, whether in business, politics or anything else, few ever managed to complete their leadership in this sterling manner.

I wish for the people of Bhutan to know how rare and precious this Kasho is in the entire written history of mankind. And I especially want the youth of Bhutan to know it, for the future of the nation is in their hands.

It is my ardent prayer that every Bhutanese citizen cherishes this final official act of their great leader. Cherish it and guard it with 'your body, speech and mind'.* Hold it high, as the precious and practicable yardstick against which to measure everything you do from now on and 'for all time to come'.*

That, I dare say, is the wisest and most satisfying reply to the 'faith and belief in the people of Bhutan'* entrusted by His Majesty the fourth Druk Gyalpo 'to look after the future of our nation …'.*

May the Heavens continue to smile on the people of Drukyul!

*Quote from the Royal Kasho

Meiko Nishimizu
Former Vice-President, The World Bank
Written on December 15, 2006
In the British Virgin Islands

A Natural Leader

I first met Crown Prince Jigme in 1966 when he arrived at Heatherdown, a well known prep school in Ascot at which I had been a pupil for two years. We were both 10 years of age and soon found we shared many of the same interests, especially in relation to the natural world and wildlife.

We slept in a dormitory of about six boys with the beds only a few inches apart; so late into the night, in hushed tones, he would tell me all about Bhutan…the high Himalayan peaks, the forested foothills, the lakes, the rivers, the Dzongs, the lamas, the creatures both real and mythological, as well as the history of his people and his family.

His passion for his country, his people and their culture was absolute and intense. It was not difficult to tell that he would rather have been at home in the mountains of the Dragon Kingdom than sitting behind a desk at a preparatory school for boys in the South of England! And who could blame him?

Nevertheless, he played a very full part in the life of the school, particularly on the sports field, and even then it was clear that here was a natural leader with a maturity of thought and manner way beyond his years.

Bhutan sounded so fascinating and wonderful that I could hardly believe that such a place actually existed. My doubts were dispelled, however, when in August 1968 I was asked to stay for four weeks as a guest of Prince Jigme and his parents, Their Majesties the King and Queen of Bhutan, and to be joined for the last two weeks by my family. Indeed

I was immediately overwhelmed by the splendour and unspoilt beauty of this most special mountain Kingdom, by the richness of its history and of its Buddhist culture, and by the friendliness and good nature of the people.

There was also a trip into the mountains at the head of the Ha Valley where we saw Blue Sheep, Musk Deer and Blood Pheasants. It was by far the most exciting thing I had ever done and still the grandest and most inspiring mountain scenery I have ever encountered as we made our way by mule, by yak and on foot along the narrow mountain paths, passing chortens at each summit that we reached. Certainly one thing that particularly struck me was the tremendous sense of humour possessed by the Bhutanese. They never stopped laughing!

I was lucky enough to visit Bhutan a second time in 1975, by which time Prince Jigme had acceded to the throne. I know that exposure to the outside world and the development needs of the country have changed Bhutan in so many ways, but I also know that throughout his time on the throne, the King quite rightly did everything he could to preserve the Bhutanese way of life. It cannot have been an easy challenge when faced with all the pressures brought to bear by the modern world.

In the intervening years I have followed events in Bhutan with interest, occasionally mixed with concern, but more often with approval and always with a sense of pride in my old Heatherdown school friend of 40 years ago.

The Hon. Charles Pearson
A Friend of Bhutan
2007

A King Remembered

It has been a remarkable privilege to have known His Majesty the fourth Druk Gyalpo for some 37 years. It was in 1970 that I was invited by Her Majesty Ashi Kesang Choden Wangchuck to help set up the Ugyen Wangchuck Academy in Paro and to teach science and mathematics to the sixteen pupils there, one of whom was a young man, then called Dasho Jigme, soon to be the fourth King. Coming from a teaching post at a large boarding school in Oxford, it was quite a culture shock to find myself living in the Paro Valley, which was a very different place in those days compared with today. However, I firmly believe young people are very much the same all over the world, and I very quickly settled into the job of teaching Dasho Jigme and his fellow pupils physics, chemistry, biology and mathematics. They were great fun to teach and like all young people, were sometimes naughty. But never wicked. They had a great sense of humour and worked hard. The future King fitted seamlessly into the class and expected in no way to be treated differently from the other pupils.

Dasho Jigme had been presented with a Japanese motorcycle, probably the first in Bhutan, and we learned about the physics of speed and acceleration by timing Dasho as he rode the motorcycle on the road between Paro and the Ugyen Wangchuck Academy. We learned some aspects of mathematics with the help of bows and arrows on the Academy football ground; and in well equipped science laboratories, we learned, through lots of practical experiments, the principles of science. I well recall a heart-stopping moment (for me!) when I handed Dasho Jigme a beaker of hydrochloric acid, and he accepted it, with usual Bhutanese good manners, on the palms of his two hands… and it almost fell over! All too soon after I left the

Ugyen Wangchuck Academy, I was saddened to learn of the untimely demise of His Late Majesty Jigme Dorji Wangchuck and realised that now Dasho Jigme, at all too young an age, would become the fourth King of Bhutan.

I returned to Bhutan in 1985 at the invitation of Her Majesty Ashi Kesang, and was honoured with an audience with my former pupil, now His Majesty the King of Bhutan. I will never forget the warmth with which I was received, and I will never forget the profound impression that His Majesty made on me in that audience. The young man I had known at the age of 16 had grown into a true and confident leader of his country: full of wisdom, dedication and a heartfelt determination to fulfil his role for the benefit of his people. I was struck, too, by His Majesty's remarkably detailed knowledge of all that was going on in the Kingdom and his considerable understanding of world affairs. From 1985 onwards, I visited Bhutan every year, and always I was shown that same warmth and hospitality from His Majesty, who I saw grow in stature and wisdom, confident in his aims and wishes for the Kingdom.

Those early experiences in the Bhutan of the 1970's – but especially the never-failing welcome, concern and human kindness which I have received through the years from His Majesty – have changed my life. In my old age I can never find words sufficient to express my heartfelt gratitude to His Majesty the fourth Druk Gyalpo.

A teacher always hopes that his pupils will turn out well. I have been so fortunate to have taught a pupil who has become a great leader and a shining light which will illuminate the future of Bhutan forever.

Michael Rutland
Former Teacher
2007

Opposite page: His Majesty the King enjoying a traditional yak dance with his people.

A Remarkable Experiment

Shortly after we arrived in Thimphu for the first time, Adrienne Clarkson (then Governor General of Canada) and I were climbing those very steep stairs, from floor to floor, for an official meeting with the King. We hadn't yet adjusted to the altitude and were puffing away, although the Bhutanese officials were careful to make us pause long enough at each landing to recover.

It was January and cold, and we were no sooner in the wonderful throne room at the top than the King noticed that we hadn't dressed for the climate inside the great building. Canadians are always convinced that it is warmer everywhere outside of Canada. His Majesty immediately called for his Mother's anti-cold remedy, which, I believe, was ginger and honey in hot water. It was certainly both hot and good. And we did warm up. As we talked, the King demonstrated that combination of nobility and informality which seems so self-evident when you meet it, but which so few other leaders ever manage.

A few days later he invited our party of Canadians to a relaxed family lunch, and as we gathered to sit down, I noticed how the King personally placed each one of us with the members of the Royal Family, until only the two most junior Canadians were left standing. Then he sat down himself and put them on either side of him. At first they were so taken aback that they didn't know what to say. But he drew them out, and they were quickly engaged in an intense conversation. Each time I see these two, they remind me of that day and their wonderful conversation.

There is a delicate balance between tradition and change, national culture and international influences, natural medicine and Western medicine, the Bhutanese talent for consensus and the Western love of debate. To create these balances is to create the expression of a remarkable experiment. It was clear to Adrienne and me as we travelled around Bhutan that the King and his father before him have been central to this whole process, just as they have been to the country's approach to everything from national dress to education.

Cultures elsewhere have felt threatened by the outside world. Instead of seeking highly original and positive balances, they have slipped into divisive fear. What we found in Bhutan was the sort of originality which comes from an equilibrium between carefully-used intelligence and calm self-confidence, with an essential dose of good humour overlaying it all. Bhutan has been very fortunate to have had such a King.

John Ralston Saul
Author
2007

People at the Centre of Development

It is with deepest respect and greatest admiration that I write this message to pay my highest tribute to His Majesty King Jigme Singye Wangchuck. Under the visionary and dynamic leadership of His Majesty the King, the Kingdom of Bhutan has clearly made tremendous achievements in the political, economic and social spheres. He has been faced with a multitude of challenges – from those dealing with security and other issues in the south to providing basic social services for the population – many of which were of a formidable nature and of great magnitude. During the 34 years of his reign, His Majesty has always led and shown his people the most appropriate path toward moving forward. Bhutan has clearly succeeded in overcoming many woes, and has rapidly made progress in nation-building, reaching many milestones and immense accomplishments.

I have always been most impressed by His Majesty's genuine care for his people and by Bhutan's development path, which places people at its very centre in the truest sense, improving their socio-economic well-being and enhancing their happiness, including spiritual happiness. This combination of economic and social development, with human development and emotional enhancement at its core, is what many countries are striving to achieve all over the world.

Some of my fondest memories of Bhutan come from many treks to the remote parts of the country. The walks and discovery of Bhutan were exhilarating and truly enjoyable. I especially valued the encounters with the people who live in these places, and they gave me lasting inspiration and strength as I learned their wisdom and outlook on life.

I was most touched on numerous occasions by the warmth and graciousness of His Majesty the King and Their Majesties the Queens. The caring words and the most kind gestures of Their Majesties were truly moving, and I am grateful beyond words for their thoughtfulness, benevolence and generosity.

May I wish His Majesty King Jigme Singye Wangchuck, His Majesty King Jigme Khesar Namgyel Wangchuck and members of the Royal Family all the prosperity and happiness for the future.

Akiko Yuge
Former UN Resident Co-ordinator
and UNDP Resident Representative in Bhutan
2007

The future of our nation lies in the hands of the Bhutanese children.

His Majesty Jigme Singye Wangchuck

Chapter Six

From a King to the People

Bhutan is stepping into a new era. The vision of the fourth Druk Gyalpo unfolds everyday as the Bhutanese people take the responsibility for the destiny of the Kingdom of Bhutan.

The journey to democracy has begun, and the legacy of a king takes shape day by day.

Above: The royal family and members of the government and armed forces at a district meeting.
Opposite page: The winds of change are blowing over the Himalayan Kingdom of Bhutan as the country moves from a monarchy to parliamentary democracy

Royal Kasho

As I had announced during the National Day celebrations last year about my abdication, and also briefed the Lhengye Zhungtshog on this decision, the time has now come for me to hand over my responsibilities to Trongsa Penlop Jigme Khesar Namgyel Wangchuck.

While we prepare ourselves for parliamentary democracy in 2008, we must all pledge with our body, speech and mind to be unwavering and steadfast in our efforts to strengthen the sovereignty and security of Bhutan, to secure the blessings of liberty, ensure justice and peace in our country, and enhance the unity, happiness and well-being of our people for all time to come.

In taking note of the progress that our nation has made over the past thirty-four years, I would like to state that whatever we have achieved so far is due to the merit of the people of Bhutan. I, therefore, wish to express my gratitude to the Clergy, the officials of the Royal Government, the members of the business community and our security forces, and to all the people of the twenty Dzongkhags for their unfailing support and loyalty to me and the country.

I am confident that a very bright and great future lies ahead for Bhutan with the leadership of a new King and democratic system of government that is best suited for our country, as enshrined under the Constitution. I have every confidence that there will be unprecedented progress and prosperity for our nation during the reign of our fifth King.

As I hand over my responsibilities to my son, I repose my full faith and belief in the people of Bhutan to look after the future of our nation, for it is the Bhutanese people who are the true custodians of our tradition and culture, and the ultimate guardians of the security, sovereignty and continued well-being of our country.

May the blessing of Ugyen Guru Rimpoche, the father of our nation Zhabdrung Ngawang Namgyal and our Guardian Deities continue to guide the destiny of our country and protect the future of the glorious Palden Drukpa.

Given at Tashichhodzong on the Twentieth Day of the Tenth Month of the Fire Dog Year, corresponding to the Ninth Day of December 2006.

Kuensel Editorial

Of Destiny

Men see the present, great men see the future. We saw this week, through our tears and smiles, the birth of a new era in history with remarkable clarity. We saw, under such extraordinary circumstances, that it represents not just an auspicious occasion for Bhutan, but a unique event in human history.

In handing over the responsibilities of state to his son and heir, Jigme Khesar Namgyel Wangchuck, His Majesty the fourth Druk Gyalpo has ushered in a new period of a dynasty that has, for 100 years, personified enlightened leadership and profound wisdom. His Majesty has ensured that Bhutan continues to be a land blessed with great leaders.

It is also a gesture of confidence in the fifth Druk Gyalpo His Majesty Jigme Khesar Namgyel Wangchuck and in a new generation of Bhutanese. We saw the continuity of a sacred legacy in the wisdom and compassion that the Crown Prince portrayed as he met with people from every corner of the country to explain the essence of the political transformation taking place today.

His Majesty the King's real gift to the nation and people is a safe, secure and happy future.

The past three decades of Bhutanese history saw the unfolding of a vision that achieved the impossible in statecraft. His Majesty Jigme Singye Wangchuck ascended the throne as a young teenager under tragic circumstances and steered the kingdom through an era of unprecedented change that represented a fine balance of tradition and modernity.

Today, landlocked Bhutan enjoys the highest per capita income in the region, a pristine environment and a balanced ecology that the world admires. Our unique values and culture, that have given us the mettle to survive dramatic social change, remain largely intact. Political stability in a turbulent world continues to ensure phenomenal all around growth. We have the institutions set in place to strengthen good governance.

As His Majesty's clear long-term vision continues to unfold we are poised for exciting change. Today's succession of the Druk Gyalpo is the first of historic transitions that will shape our future and ensure the well-being of the people for all time. We will see the adoption of the first written Constitution and, along with it, the establishment of a parliamentary democracy.

We understand, in hindsight, that His Majesty's goals were clearly planned and strategically implemented.

> *We do not mourn the departure of His Majesty as our monarch, but celebrate the achievement of his destiny*

Come 2008, we will see the start of a system of governance that has been meticulously designed for the future. It will be a polity that represents a blend of global democratic systems and Bhutan's own traditional structures to ensure the stability of a small and vulnerable country in a fast changing world.

Even if we do not comprehend the full significance of such statecraft, our recent past leaves us filled with optimism for the future. In an era of deep uncertainty around the globe, Bhutan has shown the world that there is hope for human society.

As a monarch who transcends the past, the present, and the future, His Majesty Jigme Singye Wangchuck is not departing, but leaving behind much of himself in the

Bhutanese people. If we expect His Majesty to influence changes from behind the scenes, it will not happen. But it is our responsibility to make sure that his selfless sacrifices were not made in vain and that the ultimate teaching of impermanence remains our strength.

The present generation of leaders were educated and trained and nurtured over the past decades. It was His Majesty himself who prepared the youth of Bhutan to take on the role of shaping the destiny of the kingdom. Now, given the opportunity to take the nation into the future, we celebrate the emergence of the fifth Druk Gyalpo as a comforting personification of our past and an inspiration for the years ahead.

We already see in His Majesty the King, Jigme Khesar Namgyel Wangchuck, the legacy that true greatness lies in serving the people, not in ruling over them. Ultimately, governance – and succession – is aimed at benefiting the people, and the Druk Gyalpo will continue to be the custodian of the interests of the common people. Zhung da mitshe is not a temporary arrangement, but a sacred system, and the Bhutanese people, whether they live in the pasturelands of the north, the modern cities or the sub tropical borders of the south, will continue to look to the throne for guidance and leadership.

The future, for the present generation of Bhutanese, is not a distant concept, but a reality that lies just around the corner. The year 2008 will soon be upon us with all its excitement and its pain, and we must be ready to move on with all the clarity that brought us here.

As His Majesty the fifth Druk Gyalpo takes the helm today, we know that just as yesterday was a dream of happiness, tomorrow is a vision of hope and confidence.

We do not mourn the departure of His Majesty as our monarch, but celebrate the achievement of his destiny. This is a wondrous moment in time, and we have the incredible privilege of expressing our deep gratitude and appreciation to His Majesty the fourth Druk Gyalpo, our hopes in His Majesty the fifth Druk Gyalpo and our unwavering faith in the sacred legacy that we call the Bhutanese system.

Photo: following pages © Kuensel Corporation

Kuensel Editorial, December 2006. Reprinted courtesy of Kuensel Corporation

There has never been a king like His Majesty Jigme Singye Wangchuck in our history and there will never be a greater king ever again.

To me personally, His Majesty is my king, my teacher, my inspiration and my tsawai lam (root guru).

His Royal Highness the Crown Prince, Jigme Khesar Namgyel Wangchuck in 2003

Above: His Royal Highness the Crown Prince held consultations on the draft Constitution in Kurtoe valley in Lhuentse on December 24, 2005.
Previous page: His Majesty the fourth Druk Gyalpo and His Royal Highness the Crown Prince after the investiture ceremony of the Trongsa Penlop on October 21, 2004.

Above: His Majesty the King, H.R.H Ashi Kezang Choden Wangchuck and H.R.H. Ashi Dechen Yangzom Wangchuck at Bhutan's first mock elections on April 21, 2007.
Following page: Fireworks over Trongsa Dzong to celebrate the installation of Trongsa Penlop, H.R.H. Jigme Khesar Namgyel Wangchuck in 2004.

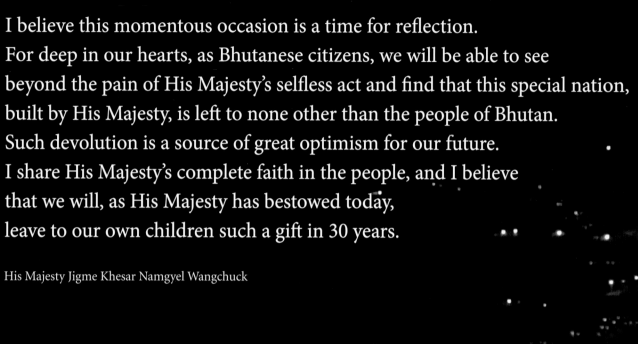

I believe this momentous occasion is a time for reflection.
For deep in our hearts, as Bhutanese citizens, we will be able to see
beyond the pain of His Majesty's selfless act and find that this special nation,
built by His Majesty, is left to none other than the people of Bhutan.
Such devolution is a source of great optimism for our future.
I share His Majesty's complete faith in the people, and I believe
that we will, as His Majesty has bestowed today,
leave to our own children such a gift in 30 years.

His Majesty Jigme Khesar Namgyel Wangchuck